Expect to be Amazed!

Expect to be Amazed!

God is the God of Romance

By Barbara Sears Nelson

Copyright © 2015 by Barbara Sears Nelson

All rights reserved. No part of this book may be used or reproduced in any manner, stored in a retrieval system, or transmitted in any form or by any means – electronic, mechanical, photocopy, recording, scanning or any other – except in the case of brief quotations in printed reviews, without the prior written permission from the Authors.

Unless otherwise indicated, all Scripture quotations are taken from the *New King James Version* ®, copyright © 1982 by Thomas Nelson, Inc. Used by permission. All rights reserved.

Scripture quotations marked AMP are taken from *The Amplified Bible, Old Testament*, copyright © 1965, 1987 by the Zondervan Corporation. *The Amplified New Testament*, copyright 1958, 1987, by the Lockman Foundation. Used by permission.

Scripture quotations marked NLT are taken from the Holy Bible, New Living Translation, copyright © 1996, 2004, 2007 by Tyndale House Foundation. Used by permission of Tyndale House Publishers, Inc., Carol Stream, Illinois 60188. All rights reserved.

Scripture quotations marked NIV are taken from the -THE HOLY BIBLE, NEW INTERNATIONAL VERSION®, NIV® Copyright © 1973, 1978, 1984, 2011 by Biblica, Inc.® Used by permission. All rights reserved worldwide.

Scripture quotations marked NCV – are taken from the New Century Version®. Copyright © 2005 by Thomas Nelson. Used by permission. All rights reserved.

Some of the names in this book have been changed for confidentially reasons.

Drawbaugh Publishing Group
444 Allen Drive
Chambersburg, PA 17202

Paperback ISBN 978-1-941746-17-2
eBook ISBN 978-1-941746-18-9

For Worldwide Distribution, Printed in the United States.

Endorsements

"The devotionals are so powerful. I love the declarations and feel encouraged in my own life and marriage, too. Some of the declarations I have been saying for my daughter who is 28 and single. There is such anointing, life, and freedom in the power of decrees and this whole book is so timely for our generation.

Thank you, Barbara Nelson, for being brave enough to jump in and write it. You write from your passion and own testimony and that gives it such authority."

Christine Tracy
Author of Tapestry - The Divine Design for Your Life
Senior Leader: Beautiful Smart Lady Summits
www.breadwineministries.com

"Barbara Nelson is a fantastic, engaging author, who addresses, with wisdom and personal experience and heart – all the crucial issues. This book is a powerful encouragement to others and an awesome fruit birthed through her perseverance and prayer.

Expect to Be Amazed! will be significant in releasing the body of Christ to walk in all that God has for us. It is encouragement not just for singles but for those *Hoping* for the promises to become a reality."

Miguel and Lisa Sanchez
Founders - Light Up Your World

"First... I just love these declarations (and I am married!) - showing us how to live by Faith with a God who knows the plans He has for us.

Second...this writing is a tool of God's hand to help show His bride, the Church, how much He loves her and is calling her to prepare for Him and His coming. #GetReady

Third…Do not underestimate small beginnings God is an amazing "multi-Tasker" so watch and be expectant. You are on a journey of destiny. No more diversions."

> Debi Tengler
> National Development Director, Arrow Child & Family Ministries,
> Speaker, Ordained minister with World Ministry Fellowship

"There are so many books on prayer that don't answer the cry, 'Yes but how?' Barbara Nelson has written an incredibly helpful devotional that answers that cry. God longs to hear from us."

> Rev Derek Rust
> Associate Evangelist, Philo Trust

Dedication

To my wonderful parents who fell in love, endured the hardships, and are enjoying the fruit of their commitment to each other, and to marriage. After many years of choosing to see the positive, to be grateful to God, praying together every day, choosing to love, choosing each other…now, they are truly living "happily ever after!"

May we all find the love of our lives, and live happily ever after, just like David and Barbara, my parents.

A note from my father to my mother found in a little black purse…

> **To my Darling Wife**
> **The Love of my life!**
> **All things are possible through Him who strengthens us.**
> **You can be all that you want to be!**
> **Love, David**

Contents

Foreword – Peter Young ... xiii
Acknowledgments ... xv
Before You Get Started - ... 1
- Now Hope Does Not Disappoint ... 1
- Is Marriage God's Will for You? ... 5
- Why Declarations? ... 9
- Write the Vision ... 13
- Instructions for the Journey ... 16

1. It is Not Good That Man Should Be Alone! ... 17
2. 1 + 1 = One ... 21
3. Let's Run! ... 25
4. Dis-Appointments ... 29
5. The Rope of Hope ... 32
6. Testimony of William and Megan ... 35
7. Mountains of Separation ... 38
8. Wisdom and the Tree of Life ... 41
9. Divine Alliances ... 45

CONTENTS

10. True Beauty	48
11. Delight to Desire	52
12. From Jealousy to Celebration	55
13. Invest in New Wineskins	58
14. A New View of Trials	62
15. Marriage is a Mission	65
16. The Woman will Encompass the Man	68
17. Woo Him, and Uncover His Feet!	72
18. Honor and Forgive	75
19. You are Worthy!	78
20. God Has Not Forgotten You	81
21. What Should I Wear?	85
22. How Will You Feel?	88
23. The Season Of Favor	91
24. Take Courage!	94
25. Now Faith	97
26. God is the God of Restoration	100
27. The Gift of Bliss	103
28. Labels: Barbie and Ken	106
29. The Right Place at the Right Time	109
30. Hawk Night Vision	112
31. Happiness! Transformed Inside Out	116
32. Expect the Best	120
33. False Summits	123
34. Believe and Receive	126

CONTENTS

35. Praying For Your Friends	130
36. What's He (She) Got?	133
37. God Delights in Prosperity	137
38. Miss Wiggy Takes a Hike	141
39. Men and Women of Strength	145
40. 40 Days of Declarations	148
Epilogue – Author's Testimony	151
The 12 Days of Christmas	153

Foreword

Peter Young

Barbara's story touches the heart. She deals with real questions, real pain, real joy, real faith, and real disappointment. Not only does she reflect transparently by firmly leaning on God's truth, but what she carries as a person will impact you. She is a woman of faith, virtue and beauty, true inner beauty. Her journey, as she looks towards God's best in marriage, will both challenge and encourage you in yours.

Indeed, all of us who were once single, or who are still single can relate to her vignettes, words of faith, stands of hope, joy, anticipation, and crushing disappointments so eloquently expressed in this devotional book. Let it touch your heart. Let it give you faith and hope. Let it prepare your heart. Laugh a little, cry a little, and reflect a lot.

In my own journey, I never dated until I met my wife in my later twenties. I remember the times of wondering, insecurity, and the path God led me on to trust Him, let go, find contentment, and be filled with security in my own identity. Then He moved. So great was God in working that when I heard a woman's voice that I had never met, my soon to be wife, at the open door of my house, my spirit leapt, my heart stopped and I knew without even setting eyes on her that I had just met the woman of my dreams! Now, after 30 years of marriage to Gwen, that amazement and wonder continues.

What about you? Are you waiting for God to move? Barbara powerfully challenges you to align your heart with God's thoughts. Her words will set your desires and faith firmly in His truth. In her 40 chapters, she includes deep and powerful declarations of faith and alignment according

FOREWORD

to God's heart. Use them as a devotional, perhaps a daily study over a couple of months.

God is big. God is amazing. Marriage is His idea. In this hour He is aligning hearts and moving mountains on behalf of His children and His advancing Kingdom. May He bless your own journey as He moves to fulfill your heart's desire.

Peter Young
Senior Leader
BridgeWay Church
Denver, Colorado

Acknowledgments

God – You tricked me into writing. Thank you for your love, wisdom and for completing the project You began. I am excited for our next adventures – and I expect to be amazed by You again.

Debi Tengler – For hearing the voice of God, and declaring this book into existence. You are my precious friend.

Peter and Gwen Young – Thank you for your apostolic vision, your wisdom, and protection as spiritual parents. Thank you for your marriage and the way you nourish our community through your love and service to each other.

Gail Horstman – Thank you for your life coaching. We have only just begun.

Angie Knowling – You are the angel who encouraged and supported me to make the big leap. Thank you.

Chris Tracy – You are a gift sent by God to edit the book, and to powerfully coach me as a writer. Thank you!

Lisa Robertson and Jennifer Miner – My sisters who always have words of wisdom, and who model great marriages to their best friends. Thank you for having so much fun in marriage.

Dean Drawbaugh – Thank you for your excellence in publishing, and for your coaching and patience in the process.

Alpha USA and Alpha International – I am so thankful Ali Hannah gave me the opportunity to work for Alpha, and to focus on the power of prayer. Ali adored his lovely wife, Nancy. Nicky and Pippa Gumbel – your love

ACKNOWLEDGMENTS

and marriage is powerful. Nicky and Sila Lee – thank you for creating the Marriage Course! And thank you Derek and Cathy Rust for your sacrifice as Marriage Course pioneers in the USA.

Ed and Ruth Silvoso – Thank you for your heart for the not-yet married, and I will never forget your prayer for me in Argentina – for my future husband! "He's coming!" Thank you also for modeling the power of a great marriage, and for your quest to transform cities and nations.

My dogs – Samson, Schuyler, and Patty. Loyal companions. I was never alone.

Introduction
Before You Get Started

Now Hope Does Not Disappoint!
"…And they lived happily ever after…."

Joy filled the atmosphere for the gorgeous wedding weekend in July at the beach. My beautiful niece, Cally, married her handsome prince, Marshall, and the celebration was filled with love, hope, joy, and promise for happily ever after.

Let me share with you the context of their wedding as it relates to my life.

My parents had just celebrated their 60th wedding anniversary, and theirs is an incredible love story. I am the youngest with a gap of seven years. My sisters married in their early 20s, my brother at 30, and between them I have 12 nieces and nephews. Cally and Marshall's wedding was the sixth celebration of one of my nieces. Because good marriages were modeled in my family, I never doubted that I would marry early in my life and have a family. Never did I imagine my nieces would get married before their Aunt Barbara.

By this sixth wedding I had gotten over the, "woe is me, the 47-year-old aunt who has not been married and can't even get a date for the wedding!" rant. Oh yes, indeed, I did have fun! No sulky aunt syndrome for this party girl. My siblings, parents, in-laws, nieces, and nephews *know* how to have a great time celebrating the miraculous event of a wedding.

Perhaps the handsome man occupying my thoughts throughout the weekend was giving me a bit of hope. After a few dates over a few months, my imagination of the potential relationship caused me to leave the post-wedding family Fourth of July celebration and fly home early. Our conversations led me to believe there was a slim possibility I could maneuver a date with this pilot.

My plan was going quite well on July 3, arriving at the airport in Denver just in time to see him in his dashing uniform. We enjoyed candlelight cocktails on his balcony in the ambience of distant fireworks, but then...his plans did not line up with *my* plan! The pilot chose to join his friends without me on the night of July 4, so I turned my attention to prepare for our big date the following night. I scurried around, preparing for a romantic mountain adventure, when the pilot called. He quickly said, "I don't think we should go out again. I just don't feel a deep connection."

Wham! Wallop! Ouch!

Rejection...again.

Disappointment...again.

Hope deferred...again.

The pilot was not the main source of my pain. He just represented all the other guys who were not my Prince Charming (either by their choice or mine). I had been praying for over 20 years for a husband, and a lot of other people had been praying for me too (including the three-year-old daughter of my niece).

Hello! God? Oh YOUUU-HOOOO! Are you forgetting about me? I think it is my turn now! I don't want to be pushy; and I think learning patience, endurance, self-control and all that stuff is great; but I think we've done enough character building by now.

With each passing wedding, and each man who chose another woman, I felt again like the fourth-grader who was the last one picked for the kickball team at recess.

Through the years I've learned I have a choice in how I respond. My response to the pilot's rejection, and the disappointment, was not to wallow in despair. I did not get mad at God and lose my faith (OK – I was frustrated with God

INTRODUCTION

for a bit); I chose to trust Him and thank Him for closing the door to a man who looked good on the surface, but who was not Mr. Right.

"Why am I not meeting a great guy?"

My personal disappointment transformed into frustration at the whole unmarried situation; not just for me, but for the many other women and men who are aching to be married to the right person. Friends all over the world, from London to Argentina to Hong Kong, are praying for the person God has for them to marry. Is there a reason so many delightful, attractive, passionate, God-loving people are not finding their marriage partner? Only God knows the answers to our questions.

After the pilot episode, in my spirit and my mind I heard the whisper of a phrase, "40 Days of Declarations." I knew I was to commit 40 days to pray for Kingdom marriages. An unction to fight the scheme of the enemy. A scheme to disable God's people through disappointments; preventing us from being the powerful people we are meant to be (or preventing us from connecting with the person we are meant to marry). My commitment was not to quiet prayers. I committed to 40 days of speaking and declaring God's powerful truth out loud over my disappointments and into the future for His Kingdom to come; His will be done, on earth as it is planned in Heaven. I invited others to join me, and a small army emerged of both women and men making declarations over Kingdom marriages.

The 40 days continued into a blog, and soon, several people were announcing their engagements. And eight months later *I* met a man! Prince Charming arrived in his trusty, beat-up old Ford. Perhaps the fulfillment of my lifelong dream of a happily-ever-after marriage was becoming a reality. Sam was the answer to so many prayers and declarations prayed over many years...or so I thought. He and I spoke of our future together, marriage, where we would live, and our exciting adventures traveling the world. I believed he was God's man for me, and my dreams were evolving into images of our life together.

More confirmation came when a woman prayed for the two of us, even suggesting we hold hands as she prayed "Your marriage will be a testimony of a Godly marriage and unity." My ring-less, unmarried left hand was on top of Sam's, but apparently she missed the telling detail.

It seemed Sam was the answer to my prayers, and I decided he was the result or outcome of the 40 days of declarations. I thought he would be my testimony. Then I could tell you that, if you did what I did, then you too would see the handsome prince ride up on his white horse (beat up Ford) and carry you off into the sunset!

After he severely found fault with my physical appearance, he drove off in the Ford without me. I thanked God for revealing the truth about Sam. His words were more painful than any relationship's end I had experienced in the past. Why did I need to go through that experience? I can see now where I ignored a few red flags, but I just did not understand, *"why?!"*

"Lean not on your own understanding…."

One thing I have learned about God is He is not a formula god. This book is not a "do this, and you will get that" kind of book. God's desire is to have an intimate relationship with us, refining us into people who love Him and trust His goodness no matter what.

The formula might be that every day, several times a day, you have a choice. Do you believe God is good? And will you choose to have faith in a good God, or will you agree with the voices of fear and doubt?

Do you choose to hope again, even when the blows of life and relationship continue to come?

After my experience with Sam, my hope, desire, and even my interest in praying for my future marriage diminished. I was experiencing the sick heart from hope deferred—extraordinary disappointment—and the last thing I wanted to do was pray about marriage. But because I made a commitment to God to compile the 40 days of emails into a book, I reluctantly returned to the project. The writing and scriptures in this book, restored my hope and belief! God used the 40 days of emails and a book project to give me firsthand experience. My hope was restored, and at the end of the 40 days, you—like me—will be amazed.

Today my prayer for you is from Romans 4:18—that like Abraham, you will again believe in *hope*.

INTRODUCTION

...who against hope believed in hope... (Romans 4:18).

When everything was hopeless, Abraham believed anyway, deciding to live not by what he saw he couldn't do but on what God said he would do (Romans 4:18, MSG).

May your hope be restored, and your heart be glad today!

Is Marriage God's Will for You?

Is it God's will for you to marry?

Now hope does not disappoint, because the love of God has been poured out in our hearts by the Holy Spirit who was given to us (Romans 5:5).

Have you asked the question?

Have you noticed some married people have been married so long they really don't remember what it is like not to be married? Occasionally they say things to those of us who are not yet married, with the intention of helping us, but clearly they have not walked in our shoes. At times like this, I feel like a cartoon character with steam erupting out of my ears. Inside, I just want to scream, but I know they simply cannot relate to my situation as they attempt to say the "right" thing. I remind myself to breathe and see their hearts and intentions are good and loving. Grace and a smile are shared, for they know not what they do or say. And, it is my responsibility to rein in my sensitivity when people ask about my marital status. It is not about them. The sting is an indication of the condition of my hurting, longing heart.

"Are you married?"

I reply positively and with faith, "Not yet!"

"Why not? Oh...you aren't into that?"

Or, "You don't like men?" (Yes, it has been said to me more than once!)

Or they say things like:

"You are just too picky!"

Or, "Have you prayed about it, and asked God if it is His will for you?"

Or, "You know, Paul said it was better to be single!"

My heart aches when I hear people say, "Well, no wonder so-and-so is not married; they are so _____." (Fill in the blank with the various criticisms shot at the people who long to be married.)

Do the opinions and judgments help? No. Careless words are abrasive to the hearts already worn down—even when the words aren't heard.

We do it—we try to find a logical reason people have not married. And the seemingly flippant words come from people who do love and care about us. To protect us from further disappointment, friends and family sometimes decide not to believe marriage is possible for us, or they search for the reasons we have not married.

It seems safer *not* to believe. There is less risk of disappointment—for them as well as for us.

One bright spring day, I was having a long-awaited coffee catch-up with a dear pastor friend. I shared with him I had been praying for marriages—for God to bring people together who are meant to be married. This is a man I consider a hero. We have been friends for many years and he has been married for most of his life. He smiled a caring *I feel sorry for you* smile, and said, "Well, that's nice, but maybe it's not God's will for you to be married. Have you prayed about it and asked God?"

Do you feel it? My jaw began to tighten to prevent my mouth from forming a terse, un-Christian response. His words stunned me, I thought he knew me and was on my side, hoping with me for the marriage of my dreams. When someone questions the desires God has passionately put on our hearts, doesn't it sound just like the serpent in Genesis speaking to Eve, "Did God really say...?"

Those are the words that began eroding marriage in the first place—doubting God's goodness and not believing His best plan.

INTRODUCTION

I remember the first time someone suggested I pray and ask God if marriage was in my future. I sincerely spent time seeking God to discern His will for me in regard to marriage. That person happened to be a young man I later prayed with about God's plan for the two of us together in marriage. Though I earnestly prayed, and I was open to an answer contrary to the desires of my heart, it became more of a religious exercise—something Christian singles need to *do*. It sounds noble and humble to seek God's will regarding marriage, but I wonder if it just causes us all to doubt.

God's answer came quickly.

Could questioning and doubting God's will for marriage cause confusion for some, and therefore hold people back from meeting their marriage partner? It is not the people who speak the words that pierce like arrows; it is the *doubt* in the words they are speaking.

Paul tells us in his letter to the Corinthians it is good to be single and celibate because you can serve God with fewer distractions. He also says if you burn with passion, then get married! (See 1 Corinthians 7:8-9, 26.) He doesn't even suggest praying about the idea.

When one of my favorite ministers, Patricia King, teaches and encourages about marriage in her conferences, she exclaims: "God is 100 percent behind your desire for marriage!"[1]

How Do We Know God's Will?

Don't copy the behavior and customs of this world, but let God transform you into a new person by changing the way you think. Then you will learn to know God's will for you, which is good and pleasing and perfect (Romans 12:2 NLT).

Is marriage God's perfect will for everyone? Maybe. I believe marriage was God's before-the-fall, perfect design for male and female. Yet, we are living after the fall. Jesus' death and resurrection broke the curse. The victory is His. We are in the time where we need to partake in enforcing His victory.

You have a choice to believe marriage is God's best will for most or all of His people. I believe marriage is the image of God—male and female—united as one.

1 + 1 = One!

There is incredible supernatural power when a husband and wife agree in prayer and it is a power that is underutilized and not understood. If the union *wasn't* powerful, the enemy would not be working so hard to break up Christian marriages.

If there is such intense spiritual warfare around Christian marriages—even with so many books and ministries designed to help people stay married—why wouldn't the enemy also be working to *prevent* these marriages?

Several years after I began wondering these things, I discovered someone who agreed with me, and she referred me to the resources of Arthur Burk who has a teaching called *Releasing Singles*.

> **You are a beautiful, intelligent, competent, gracious, and godly Christian. So why are you still single?**
>
> **There is a concerted demonic assault against godly families. One facet of that battle is to keep godly women (and men) from marrying.**
>
> **Arthur Burk, Releasing Singles[2]**

I felt a stronger unction to pray for marriages for the not-yet married. It was not about little ol' me anymore!

> **One of the ways the enemy is attacking Christian Marriages is by keeping people alone and single. Patricia King[3]**

Esther was appointed, "for such a time as this." (See Esther chapters 1 and 4.) In the first chapter of Esther, the marriage of Persian King Aheurses and Queen Vashti fell apart because of rebellion, selfishness, hard-heartedness, anger, and a bit too much alcohol in the mix. This left the kingdom fragile.

INTRODUCTION

The king needed a new queen, and since he did not have Match. com, eHarmony, or Christian Mingle at the time, his servants gathered a group of eligible women for the king to select from.

After a year of physical and spiritual preparation—and most likely much prayer—Esther was the lovely lady who captivated the king, chosen out of many other young women as his new queen. Esther was unaware the marriage was a divine alliance. God had a plan much bigger than Esther could imagine, and the lives of many Jews depended on her submission to God's plan and her marriage to the king.

You have picked up this book, decided to try something new, and, like Esther, you have been called "for such a time as this." Like the salts and oils polished and prepared Esther, the rough and hardened places in your heart will become soft and pliable as you read and declare. Just as Esther bathed in perfumes, you will be washed and transformed with God's Word. Through this journey, you will become a sweet fragrance to your beloved. Even if you meet that person tomorrow, these prayers and declarations will nourish you and your future marriage.

Remember, your praying and declaring is not just for you. Praying through this book has the potential to impact and transform your sphere of influence, strengthening existing marriages and supernaturally connecting many people with a desire for marriage.

Why Declarations?

Three weeks after their first date, my father proposed and my mother said, "What took you so long?" My parents' marriage is a testimony, as we say in our family, "God is the God of romance!" They are madly in love at age 88 and 91, and, after more than 60 years of marriage, the love they have cultivated and share is a love we hope to experience in marriage. As romantics, they have been instrumental in connecting several lonely hearts to their marriage partner.

A mother's heart aches when the marriage of her child is delayed or destroyed. My mother, affectionately known as Babby, tried to help God with my unmarried situation on occasion. Prayer was the best activity for my concerned mom, and she spent years praying with my father for our family, and for my future husband and me to meet.

Some of my mother's famous quotes:

> **Onward and upward!**
>
> **Pick yourself up, dust yourself off, and start all over again!**
>
> **Be careful of what you say—your words are powerful!**

So when my mother taught me there was supernatural power when we speak the Word and promises of God, or when we utter negative things about ourselves or others, I listened. In recent years, many Christian teachers I respect have been catching up to my mother's wisdom with a similar message—our words have power to create, good or bad.

A few years ago, a book was handed to me after a lovely dinner party at the home of a married couple, whom I introduced. Charles Capps' *Faith and Confession* reminded me of my mother's words of wisdom, and has inspired me to pray differently about my wishes for marriage. When I told my mother about my discovery of Charles Capps, she said, "Oh yes, I heard him preach many times!" The same teaching that influenced my mother's life is now impacting mine. Isn't God fun?

> **God's principles are involved in confession and the principles of faith. The Bible says "faith comes by hearing, and hearing by the Word of God." It didn't say that's the only way we can get faith.**
>
> **God's word that is conceived in the heart, formed with the tongue, and spoken out of the mouth becomes a spiritual force, releasing the ability of God.**[4]

So, if speaking or declaring the Word of God regarding our desires for marriage is a supernatural force releasing faith, hope and God's ability, would you agree it's worth stepping out of your routine and trying something new? I

INTRODUCTION

believe as we choose to make declarations agreeing with each other, for each other, and for people all over the world longing for a Godly marriage, we will see an increase in marriages.

> **Death and life are in the power of the tongue,**
>
> **And those who love it will eat its fruit**
>
> **(Proverbs 18:21).**

I have taught on declarations for years and have heard testimony after testimony of how adding this habit has been transformational to all kinds of people. I'm so convinced of the power of declarations to unlock destiny. Steve Backlund[5]

Prophetic declarations release God's power to bring about change in our lives! Kris Vallotton[6]

The Kingdom of God is "voice activated." When God created, He spoke things into existence. Your decrees of the words contained in God's covenant are powerful and they create realms of blessing. Patricia King[7]

When the devil keeps on asking you to look at your past, there must be something good in the future he doesn't want you to see. Keep your hand on the plow and keep looking straight ahead! I rehearse godly beliefs and declarations every day. How about you? James Goll[8]

My pastor, Peter Young, of BridgeWay Church in Denver, Colorado, teaches the following about declarations:

1. Declarations are the people of God agreeing with God's purposes.
2. We are reaching forward and pulling the future into the present.
3. We are aligning ourselves with God's Word and promises.
4. A declaration is making a statement saying, *this is not negotiable!*

Pastor Peter's teaching on declarations confirms the importance of each of us making declarations together. When we come into agreement, and speak the powerful Word of God out loud, we are pulling the promises of God into our lives and the lives of others. *His Kingdom come!*

The important thing to remember is this is not just for your own self-serving desire, but another person is out there longing to marry *you*! It is the God-designed destiny for both of your lives—and many others.

> **Mark Twain once said, "Take your mind out every now and then and dance on it. It is getting all caked up." That was his way of saying: try something new, break new ground, get out of your rut. John Maxwell[9]**

By embarking on this journey of making declarations for marriages, you are choosing to believe—to trust God; to grow in faith; and to grab onto the rope of hope.

You are choosing to allow God and His powerful Word to heal your heart from the battering of disappointments and hope deferred.

You are choosing to tell disappointment, fear, and discouragement to *hit the road, get lost, be gone!*

I am not promoting a formula of *do this and you will get married and live happily ever after*. But I *am* saying *all things are possible with God*. At the least, you will build up your faith, increase hope and peace, and have more joy in the Lord.

> **You will also DECLARE a thing, and it will be established for you. So light will shine on your ways (Job 22:27).**

Declarations for Today:

Wait on the Lord; Be of good courage; And He shall strengthen your heart; Wait, I say, on the Lord! (Psalm 27:13-14).

May the God of your hope so fill you with all joy and peace in believing [through the experience of your faith] that by the power of the Holy Spirit you may abound and be overflowing (bubbling over) with hope (Romans 15:13 AMP).

INTRODUCTION

Believe that you will see the goodness of the Lord in the land of the living (Psalm 27:13).

Do not lose heart. Let's endeavor together to bubble over with hope.

We are on a journey to pray for many more people to experience *happily ever after*, just as my parents are experiencing today.

Write the Vision

And then God answered:

"Write this.

"Write what you see. Write it out in big block letters so that it can be read on the run. This vision-message is a witness pointing to what's coming. It aches for the coming—it can hardly wait! And it doesn't lie. If it seems slow in coming, wait. It's on its way. It will come right on time" (Habakkuk 2:2-3 MSG).

I believed God had given me signs it was His plan I marry a certain man. Blake and I agreed to pray and fast; to ask God for direction regarding marriage. For a few years I kept seeing "signs" I thought meant God was confirming that he was my future husband. Why wasn't Blake getting the same message? I think Christian women in particular fall into a trap of focusing on one man, even when their romantic interest is not reciprocated. We look for signs from God that he or she is "the one" when it isn't God's plan. This is a trap and it leads to idolatry. It keeps us focused on a fantasy, prevents us from being free and open to the Lord or anyone else; and it becomes an obsession.

After years of holding onto my imagined signs that I would marry Blake, my illusions disappeared when I was asked, "Take God out of your situation, and what do you have?"

My answer: *No romance, only an obsession and wishful thinking.*

The Bible tells us to write the vision of the desires of our hearts. I have changed my mind on what writing the vision means regarding my future husband and marriage. In the past, people suggested I write a list of the qualities I desire in a husband, including his height, hair, occupation, etc. And I may have met that guy a few times, but he was not the man God planned for my Kingdom marriage. He looked good on the surface, but lacked the character or moral compass to accompany me on the journey.

After reading *The Slight Edge*, where author Jeff Olsen explains turning your dreams into a reality, I followed his instructions and wrote the vision for five areas of my life. Consequently, my "future husband list" changed from eye-candy to character qualities. What ensued was a vision for the *purpose* of our marriage.

This is what Olsen says:

> The most critical skill of achieving success in any area from sports to finance, radiant health to fulfilling relationships, is the skill of envisioning. Envisioning something simply means having the ability to create a vivid picture of something that hasn't actually happened yet, and make that picture so vivid that it feels real. Envisioning doesn't happen simply by creating a picture in your mind. If your dreams and aspirations are happening in your mind only, that's not envisioning, that's wishful thinking.
>
> You need to write it down. Making pictures of it, which people sometimes call a "dream board," is even better. Speaking it out loud is the most powerful of all. But at the very least, write it down. The moment you do, it has started to become real.[10]

Shake off the dust! Dare to dream!

I asked a group of friends what they thought about writing out the characteristics of the men we would like to marry. Some answers were things like *yes…it's risky…even scary. We might be disappointed. Wouldn't it be easier to pray "God, Your will be done, and I trust You to send the right man to me?"* We agreed there was a valid reason to "write the vision" of our desires.

Writing the vision will prevent us from settling for less than God's best, and those red flags will be easier to discern when someone comes along who is not meant for us.

INTRODUCTION

Charles Capps in his book *Faith and Confession* writes:

> **Hope is a goal setter. You must have a goal…a goal gives direction…. Faith is the substance of things hoped for.**
>
> **Hope works in the head. What you continue to speak becomes your goal. Your head is the goal-setter. Where there is no hope, there is no goal set for the better—although "no hope" sets a negative goal.**[11]

Let's Get Started

1. Write the vision of how God sees you. Take some time to write the vision God has for you. What is He saying about you? He loves and adores you, and you need to remind your spirit, mind, and heart of how incredible you are. (See Appendix A for a list of scriptures.) God says you are beautiful, powerful, a wife of valor, a man of strength. You are clothed in His righteousness, you are His heir, and His beloved son or daughter. Write the vision. Write it all out, this is an important step. You will add to the list as you go through this book.

2. Pray and ask God to give you His vision for your future spouse and marriage. Describe the person you envision yourself marrying; the relationship; the marriage. God may change it up a little, but only to surprise you "exceedingly, abundantly above all you can ask or think!" (See Ephesians 3:20.)

My friend, Sally, married a man who is the physical opposite of the tall, dark and handsome men she had always dated in her past. Though he may *look* different than her ideal picture of a man, she is one of the happiest married ladies I know. She adores her husband. He loves her, honors her, and respects her. They have a wonderful marriage—full of love, laughter and joy. Did she have a list? I don't know, but I do know she desired to meet a man passionate about pursuing a relationship with Jesus Christ. I know she desired a man of intelligence and wit, and God knew the desires of Sally's heart.

Instructions for the Journey

This book is arranged as a devotional to take you through 40 days of making declarations for marriages. Here are suggestions to get you started:

1. There are declarations for each day of the 40 days. This book is designed to give you freedom to go through it quickly in 40 days, or to take your time.
2. Use the 12 Days of Christmas section to encourage you though the Christmas season.
3. Create a "Vision Bookmark" or index card, and write your visions and dreams to keep them in front of you. I encourage you to declare your vision often—daily or weekly.
4. Gather one or more friends to pray with over the 40 days.
5. Expect to be amazed!

Day 1
It is Not Good that Man Should be Alone

Glorious hats designed to fascinate; dashing morning coats; royal horses elegant with every step—no, it was not Derby Day. On April 29, 2011, I was glued to the incredible royal wedding of Kate and William. Though not a royal wedding junkie like some of my friends who were out of bed at 3 a.m. with tea and scones, I *was* drawn to the pomp and circumstance and remained in front of my TV much longer than I planned. What I observed was the beginning of a new era for the royal family—a global celebration offering a symbol of hope—and I wondered if this wedding was a sign of God restoring marriages throughout the earth. I felt something needed to be done to cause a shift and a new beginning for marriage in God's Kingdom family, and I kept hearing in my mind, *"the Lord God said 'It is not good for the man to be alone!'"* (See Genesis 2:18 NIV.)

I love researching the definitions of biblical words, and for the first time I looked up the word "alone." I was astonished to see that the Hebrew word is "bad." And the first definition is "separation."

Strong's #905: **bad**, bad; from 909; prop. Separation; by impl. A part of the body, branch of a tree, bar for carrying; fig. Chief of a city; espec. (with prep. Pref.) as adv., aprt, only, besides:- alone, apart, bar, besides, branch, by self, of each alike, except, only, party, staff, strength.

The word, "man," in Genesis 2:18 is "adam," and it is one of the four Hebrew words for man. That word, "man," is translated "humankind, male, and female." Therefore, God said it is not good for man *or* woman to be alone.

God says that man (humankind) alone is bad. *Bad!*

Cindy Jacobs wrote in her book, *Women of Destiny*: "The only thing God said was not good in all of creation was man's aloneness. (See Gen. 1:4, 10, 12, 18, 21, 25, 31; cf. Gen. 2:18.) Therefore, it stands to reason that Satan would want to wound the relationships between men and women, not only in the home, but also in the workforce and Church, so man would once again be in the only state God called 'not good.'"[1]

Because it is *bad*!

Marriage began with Adam and Eve. God placed them in the Garden with instructions for their life together.

> **Then God blessed them, and God said to them, "Be fruitful and multiply; fill the earth and subdue it; have dominion over the fish of the sea, over the birds of the air, and over every living thing that moves on the earth" (Genesis 1:28).**

My Bible says it like this:

God created man to be His kingdom agent, to rule and subdue the rest of creation, including the aggressive satanic forces, which would soon infringe upon it[2].

> **Then the rib which the Lord God had taken from man He made (built) into a woman,** *and He brought her to the man.* **(See Genesis 2:22.)**

The New American Standard version says, "The Lord *fashioned* into a woman...."

Marriage was God's idea. He formed man, then fashioned or "built" woman, and God brought the woman to the man—the woman who was to be his wife. When Adam saw her, he recognized her, and may have exclaimed, "Whoa – man! Good job, God!"

One of my prayers for the man God has chosen for me is that he will recognize me as his wife. I pray his spirit, and mine, will leap with recognition, and the knowing in our spirits will surpass or override our minds and reason.

DAY 1

It is not good for man and woman to be alone, *but God*—"All things work together for good, for those who love Him, and are called according to His purposes" (Romans 8:28). I do not feel incomplete as a person, but my heart and spirit long for the completeness of God's design for us as men and women, and the power of that unity.

One of my not-yet married male friends wrote in an email to me: "I have always conceded that we were built for marriage and anything less falls short of the reflection of God that we are called to be." He went on to explain his view of marriage as man and woman are designed to refine each other as we bring together male and female, mirroring the fullness of God.

The strength and power of a Christian marriage is much bigger than we can comprehend, which is the reason for so much warfare around marriages. Satan hates the power of men and women in unity because it is the mysterious, glorious image of God.

When we speak the promises of God, we will create change. Made in the image of God, our words have the power to create. The Word of God is *powerful*, and speaking His Word out loud will build your faith. *"Faith comes by hearing!"* (See Romans 10:17.) In order to hear, you need to speak.

> **Do not remember the former things,**
>
> **Nor consider the things of old.**
>
> **Behold, I will do a new thing,**
>
> **Now it shall spring forth;**
>
> **Shall you not know it?**
>
> **I will even make a road in the wilderness**
>
> **And rivers in the desert (Isaiah 43:18-19 NKJV).**
>
> **The man who finds a wife finds a treasure, and he receives favor from the Lord (Proverbs 18:22 NIV).**

Declarations:

Thank you Father God for this journey of faith and hope, to see Your Kingdom come on Earth as it is in Heaven! On behalf of the men and women You have appointed to come together for Your purposes in marriage:

1. Even when there was no reason for hope, Abraham kept hoping – believing in the God who brings the dead to life and who creates new things out of nothing. I declare marriage is God's plan for my life! (See Romans 4:17 NLT.)
2. We declare God is doing a new thing, and it shall spring forth *now*. (See Isaiah 43:18.)
3. *"He who finds a wife finds a treasure, and obtains favor from the Lord"* (Proverbs 18:22). Open the eyes of the men's hearts, so they will find their wives, their treasure, and the men will obtain the favor of God.
4. We declare that we are available: As women, to be presented to the men of God whom You have chosen to be our husbands. Present us to Your *best* men. As men, to be open to receive the woman God is bringing to us. Present us with Your *best* woman.
5. We receive the favor of Esther, and the kings will be attracted to the women You have ordained as their wives more than any other women. Give all of us an overwhelming, unwavering attraction for Your best for each of us.
6. We declare a blessing of favor over the marriages we know and love. Lord, impart to them a fresh recognition of each other, and restore that leap in their hearts and spirits for each other. What God has brought together, protect and strengthen by Your refreshing Spirit—and let nothing separate.
7. We declare *no* weapon formed against our marriages—present or future—will prosper! (See Isaiah 54:17.)

Amen! Expect to be amazed!

Day 2
1+1=One

Weddings are a day of hope, joy, giddy love, promise, and expectancy for a bright new future.

My nephew, Willis, was married on a Saturday in February to the incredible and beautiful Caitlin. Their wedding was a testimony and a reminder that God is the God of romance! He does do exceedingly abundantly above all that we can ask or think. (See Ephesians 3:20.)

It is difficult to describe the sense I felt during the wedding celebration. A stirring in my spirit said the gifts of romance, love, hope, faith, and joy were available to all who were willing to receive them.

In rejoicing with those who rejoice, new hope and faith for an "exceedingly abundantly above" romance can be imparted to those who delight themselves in the Lord and celebrate at the wedding banquet.

When my nieces, Laura and Elizabeth, sisters of the groom, read Romans 12:9-15 during the service, I was reminded of the royal wedding of William and Kate. The same scripture was read over the Royals, followed by an extraordinary message given by the Bishop of London. (See Appendix B).

The Bishop began by reading Romans 12:9-15:

> **Let love be without hypocrisy. Abhor what is evil. Cling to what is good. Be kindly affectionate to one another with brotherly love, in honor giving preference to one another; not lagging in diligence, fervent in spirit, serving the Lord; rejoicing in hope, patient in**

> tribulation, continuing steadfastly in prayer; distributing to the needs of the saints, given to hospitality....
>
> Rejoice with those who rejoice, and weep with those who weep." (See Romans 12:9-15.)
>
> Be who God meant you to be and you will set the world on fire. Marriage is intended to be a way in which man and woman help each other to become what God meant each one to be; their deepest and their truest selves.
>
> In a sense, every wedding is a royal wedding with the bride and groom as king and queen of creation, making a new life together so life can flow through them into the future. (See Appendix B).

As Christians, we are part of God's Kingdom, and through our marriages, we release life and love into the world around us.

> Then God said, "Let Us [Father, Son and Holy Spirit] make mankind in Our image, after Our likeness, and let them have complete authority over the fish of the sea, the birds of the air, the [tame] beasts, and over all the earth, and over everything that creeps upon the earth."
>
> So God created man in His own image, in the image and likeness of God He created him; male and female He created them (Genesis 1:26-27 AMP).
>
> God blessed them; "Prosper! Reproduce! Fill Earth! Take charge!" (Genesis 1:28 MSG)

When I read the above verses, I see the image of God partnering with the union of man and woman. A Kingdom marriage is two people becoming one to fulfill the great commission. As my friend Lynda would say: "It is a co-mission, not a uni-mission."

> "Kingdom marriage is entered into not for its own sake, not simply because of love or companionship or even the raising of a family—

but for a ministry partnership, something to enhance both the husband and wife's ability to give themselves effectively to the work of the Kingdom of God." Unknown[1]

My friend, Peyton notes:

"I once heard someone say that Kingdom marriages are set aside to a specific purpose that neither the husband nor wife can do alone. It's amazing to think that, while God has incredible paths for me as an individual and as a woman, there are some things that can only be fulfilled through this Kingdom marriage. For me, it was an 'ah-ha' moment of how important this is—on a larger scale than just being married to the right guy. I think of Adam and Eve, and Abraham and Sarah. Each had their own relationship with God, and yet, they received promises and a purpose that could only be fulfilled together."

Declarations:

Thank you, Father God, that we have been adopted as Your sons and daughters into Your Kingdom that has no end. Thank you for giving us a greater revelation of what it means to be Your royal children as we make these declarations.

1. I declare I am royalty because I am a child of the King of kings. "For all who are led by the Spirit of God are children of God. So I have not received a spirit that makes me a fearful slave. Instead, I received God's Spirit when He adopted me as his child. Now I call him, 'Abba, Father.' For His Spirit joins with our spirits to affirm that we are God's children" (Romans 8:14-16 NLT).
2. I declare that I receive the first mandate given to man and woman from God, and I will: "Prosper! Reproduce! Fill the Earth!" And "Take charge!" (See Genesis 1:28 MSG.)
3. I declare that I will seek first the Kingdom of God, and as I focus on the King of kings, all the things I need in life, (including a spouse), will be given to me. (See Matthew 6:33.)

4. I declare that I have been called "for such a time as this," to join in partnership and marriage with the person God has chosen for me. (See Esther 4:14.)
5. I declare that *all* things are working together for *good*, because I love God, and I am called according to His Kingdom purposes. (See Romans 8:28.)
6. I declare that I believe, and *all* things are possible with God. (See Mark 9:23.)
7. I declare that I do not fear, for it is my Father's good pleasure to give me the Kingdom. (See Luke 12:32.)

Amen! Expect to be amazed!

Day 3
Let's Run!

You will also declare a thing, and it will be established for you. So light will shine on your ways (Job 22:28).

Crossing the threshold of each new year, or month, or week, or even a new endeavor like this, I envision myself taking off heavy garments that have been dragging me down in past seasons. I then receive new hope and fresh vision for the future—lighter and more empowering garments. It's a *new* day. I do not want anything to hinder me from the promises of our faithful God.

When I began this project of making declarations over marriages, I was eager to step out of the past years with their disappointments and unfulfilled promises. Before charging into the new adventure, I took time to reflect on all the wonderful things God has done in my life, rather than on what I perceived to be missing.

God *is good*, and challenges are all part of the story—my testimony. I am so grateful.

I urge you, too, to reflect on God's goodness in your life and His faithfulness as you begin this journey.

What do you need to leave in the past? There is no reason to dwell on disappointments. It may be enlightening to be aware of anything that hinders your progress towards deeper relationships, including your relationship with Jesus.

Therefore, since we are surrounded by such a huge crowd of witnesses to the life of faith, let us strip off every weight that slows us down,

> especially the sin that so easily trips us up. And let us run with endurance the race God has set before us (Hebrews 12:1 NLT).

Sometimes we need to leave the *familiar* behind, because often the familiar things we've allowed to hang out with us are doubt, unbelief, fear, discouragement, and self-pity. They become comfortable because we know them so well. Making declarations is transforming your mind, and the old mindsets, opinions and expectations need to be locked away in the past season of your life. It can be scary to step out in faith and into the unknown; into a new, confident identity. You will experience uncomfortable pangs of a new training regimen, but continue to move forward. Step out of the boat!

> **Now the LORD had said to Abram: "Get out of your country, from your family and from your father's house, to a land that I will show you" (Genesis 12:1).**

Ruth also left her homeland, her country, her family, and her father's house.

> **So she (Ruth) fell on her face, bowed down to the ground, and said to him (Boaz), "Why have I found favor in your eyes, that you should take notice of me, since I am a foreigner?"**

> **And Boaz answered and said to her, "It has been fully reported to me, all that you have done for your mother-in-law since the death of your husband, and how you have left your father and your mother and the land of your birth, and have come to a people whom you did not know before.**

> **"The LORD repay your work, and a full reward be given you by the LORD God of Israel, under whose wings you have come for refuge" (Ruth 2:10-12).**

As we enter this new adventure, let us leave old and familiar disappointments and patterns in the past. You may even need to step away from voices of people who are close to you who may have quietly lost hope in your future marriage. Close the doors and receive new garments woven with gold; the glory of God.

DAY 3

It is time to do something different, rewire your mindsets and subconscious beliefs, and run with the expectancy of seeing the long-awaited promises fulfilled.

Are you ready? – Let's *run*!

Declarations:

Lord God Almighty, King of kings: Thank you for a fresh beginning! I pray that every person reading this, and those for whom we are praying, will be filled with the spirit of wisdom and revelation in the knowledge of Jesus; and the light of Christ will shine on, and reveal *all* things we need to shed or leave behind. Thank you Lord that You are faithful!

1. We declare that we choose to strip off every weight that has been slowing us down – especially the sin that so easily trips us up or entangles us. Father God, reveal the weights and the sin in our lives now. (Pause and allow the Holy Spirit to speak to your spirit.) Lord Jesus, reveal to us the "familiar" things we need to leave behind, and give us the courage to pack up and *go*!
2. We declare that we have the faith of Abraham, and we have ears to hear the voice of God when He says to us, *"get out!"* Lord Jesus, reveal to us any unhealthy "friendships" or relationships.
3. We declare we are getting out of any relationships that are holding us captive. (See Appendix C on breaking soul ties.)
4. We declare we are making room in our lives for God's *best*! And I declare my life is a life of order – in my home, finances, health, and spiritual life. What are the things you need to do to make room for your Kingdom marriage partner? Clean out your closets in your home and in your heart! Ask God to show you how today.
5. We declare that we receive divine favor, just as Ruth and Boaz received the favor of God that attracted one to the other. We receive the full reward. We receive the person God has appointed as our marriage partner.
6. *Women*: We declare that our kings greatly desire our beauty, and we put on the garments for the New Year, woven with gold. (See Psalm 45:13.)

Men: Desire is increasing in me, and in men throughout this world. We greatly desire the beauty of the wives God has for us. (See Psalm 45:11.)

7. Thank you, Lord, for Your goodness and faithfulness to run with us; to transform us by the renewing of our minds through the power of Your Word.

Amen! Expect to be amazed!

Day 4
Dis-Appointments

The handsome 52-year-old man, not yet married, was succumbing to the manipulation of disappointment, agreeing with the lies of the accuser. He told himself "I've decided that God does not want me to be married so I am not even going to try anymore." Because he had not yet found his wife, he decided God was withholding good things from him, and he chose *not* to hope for happily-ever-after.

I believe he *will* be married, and I pray for him to find a wife. He chose to speak words opposite the promises of God, and thus he reinforced lies. We all do that. Sometimes it feels easier to give up. We give in to the negative beliefs that God is not good and is withholding the gift of a wife or husband; or that marriage is not God's plan for our life.

We have all been disappointed in relationships and disgruntled with God, because we expected Him to cause our lives to look differently than they do.

This is what Francis Frangipane says:

> Disappointment is not just a sad, emotional state of mind; deep disappointment actually can sever our hearts from faith. It is the enemy's work. Demonically manipulated disappointment can actually "dis-appoint" a person from God's destiny for their lives.
>
> Satan can stop our destiny if we accept the power of disappointment into our lives. Once we accept the heaviness of a deep dis-appointment, backsliding is often not far away. You see, dis-appointment cuts us off from our vision, and without a vision people perish.[1]

But God says:

> Now *hope* does not disappoint, because the love of God has been poured out in our hearts by the Holy Spirit who was given to us (Romans 5:5).

> Then you will know that I am the LORD; *those who hope in Me will not be disappointed* (Isaiah 49:24 NIV).

> Now may the *God of hope* fill you with all joy and peace in believing that you may abound in hope by the power of the Holy Spirit (Romans 15:13).

Hope in the Lord does not disappoint. Hope keeps us on track with our destiny. As we have declared, the Lord is doing a new thing. It's time to turn your gaze from the past dis-appointments and look forward, eagerly expecting and anticipating God to do great things in your life.

One of my business mentors, David Byrd, says we need to "discipline our disappointments." When we discipline the disappointment, we are in control, not the disappointment. We take thoughts captive, turn them around, and speak hope and truth over the discouraging incident. It may start by being demonically manipulated, but we have the authority to take control, and manipulate our thoughts back to powerful hope in our God who is so good!

Declarations:

Lord God Almighty, thank you for Your power that works in and through us to break the chains of disappointment. We choose life, letting go and releasing the past so we are free to run into the future without hindrance.

1. We declare and decree the God of hope fills us now with all joy and peace in believing, and we abound in hope by the power of the Holy Spirit. (See Romans 15:13.)
2. We declare that *now* hope does not disappoint because the love of God was poured out in our hearts by the Holy Spirit. (See Romans 5:4-6.)

3. The perfect love of God casts out all fear, so we declare we are men and women who *fear not!* (See 1 John 4:18.)
4. For God declares He knows the plans He has for each of us; plans to prosper us and not to harm us; plans to give us a *hope* and a future. (See Jeremiah 29:11 NIV.)
5. We declare no unbelief or distrust will make us waver (doubtingly question) concerning the promises of God, but we grow strong, and we are empowered by faith, and we give praise and glory to God. (See Romans 4:20 AMP.)
6. We are fully satisfied and assured that God is able and mighty to keep His word and do what He has promised! (See Romans 4:21 AMP.)
7. We declare: the Lord God will help us; therefore we will not be disgraced; therefore we set our faces like a flint, and we know that we will not be ashamed. (See Isaiah 50:7.)

The man who decided God was not giving him a wife is now engaged to be married. He is absolutely amazed!

Amen! Expect to be amazed!

Day 5
The Rope of Hope

There are days when I feel my hope wane, subtly at first, and I begin to entertain my weariness from waiting. Then disappointment comes knocking at my door to join the fun. Those two, weariness and disappointment, pretend to be comforting "friends." But in reality they want to camp out for the pity-party to get us derailed again, focusing on what we don't have rather than the hope we do have. *"For You are my hope, O Lord God..."* (Psalm 71:5).

Thankfully, He *is* our hope. God will send a message or a friend to throw us a lifeline when we are swirling down into the pit; or when the pity party is turning into a huge event.

I always get a big dose of hope and courage at my church. Not only from the preaching, but also from people like my friend, Lynda, who is a perceptive intercessor, amazing artist, and another companion on this journey. Lynda will say hope-filled, encouraging words, full of vision: "I know the old season is over and the new is beginning. Now is the time for the breakthrough. We are going to begin to see the answers to the prayers we have been praying for years!"

We need those lifelines, the ropes of hope to take our focus off ourselves and put it back onto the God who has a great plan for our lives.

The definition for *hope* in my Spirit Filled Life Bible is worth sharing:

> **Hope, tiqvah; Strong's #8615; Hope; expectation; something yearned for and anticipated eagerly; something for which one waits. Tiqvah comes from the verb qavah, meaning "to wait for" or "to look hopefully" in a particular direction. Its original meaning was "to stretch like a**

rope." Tiqvah occurs 33 times in Josh 2:18, 21, it is translated "line" or "cord"; Rahab was instructed to tie a scarlet tiqvah (cord or rope) in her window as her hope for rescue. Yahweh Himself is the hope of the godly (Psalm 71:5). In Hosea 2:15, God's blessing on His land will transform the Valley of Achor ("trouble") into the "door of hope." [1]

Hope is waiting, eager, confident, and expectant. It is not focusing on the missing things, or yourself, it is looking out and beyond with excitement. You cannot see it yet, but you know it's coming!

It won't be long now, he's on the way! He'll show up most any minute! (Hebrews 10:36 MSG).

Remember what God has done in your life and the lives of the people you love. Thanking God, a heart of gratitude, reading the Bible, and speaking the Word out loud will pull us out from the grip of nasty disappointments and restore our hope. When you need a double portion of hope, make the following declarations and send disappointment and weariness back to the pit from where they came.

Instead of shame and dishonor, you will enjoy a double share of honor. You will possess a double portion of prosperity in your land, and everlasting joy will be yours (Isaiah 61:7 NLT).

Return to the stronghold, you prisoners of hope. Even today I declare that I will restore double to you (Zechariah 9:12).

"In the world's system, suffering produces despair. But in the Kingdom, suffering produces hope. Suffering is believing what God says long enough until what God says happens. That suffering produces something in you called perseverance." Bob Hazlett[2]

Declarations:

Thank you, Father God, for the Rope of Hope, Jesus Christ. He is our hope! Thank you for imparting each of us with fresh hope today, and the encouragement that we are not alone on this journey. Thank you, Father God, for reminding us of Your faithfulness, and for sending true friends at the perfect moment when we need to hear a word of hope. Deploy Your messengers of hope to all of us when we need to be encouraged.

1. We declare God knows the plans He has for us; plans to prosper us and not to harm us; plans to give us a hope and a future. (See Jeremiah 29:11 NIV.)
2. We declare we have returned to the stronghold of security and prosperity, for we are prisoners of hope! (See Zechariah 9:12 AMP.)
3. We agree with the declaration of the Lord God, that we will be repaid double for all of our troubles. Two blessings for each of our troubles. (See Zechariah 9:12 NLV.)
4. Jesus, You are the door of hope. We agree and declare the Lord will turn the Valley of Achor (troubling) into a door of hope and expectation. (See Hosea 2:15 AMP.)
5. We declare that instead of shame and dishonor, we will enjoy a double share of honor. (See Isaiah 61:7.)
6. We declare we will possess a double portion return, the double restoration of our inheritance, for everything that has been stolen, or everything we forfeited in the past season. (See Isaiah 61:7.)
7. We declare that everlasting *joy* is ours!

Hold on, and dare to hope!
Amen! Expect to be amazed!

Day 6

Testimony of William and Megan and the Divine X-Factor

After many years of divorce and being a single dad, there were many times I had given up hope of finding that special woman who would open my heart to a future marriage. There were many days where it was just difficult to see the future and fully trust God with the present.

I have just been blown away by the woman God had for me all along. Her story is so wonderful—about the difficult waiting she went through as well—and how gradually it became so clear that we were just meant to be a couple. So worth waiting for!

I am so grateful for the friends who have stood beside me and encouraged and prayed for me. Like the men and women from the 40 Days of Declarations Group, and others who have been so faithfully praying for Christian marriage. Thank you!

Thank you, God, for answering my prayers and the prayers of all these people.

William

Amazing!

William and Megan have a testimony. And from their testimony, we can have hope for our future. When I was sending emails at the beginning of the 40 Days of Declaration project, William was the one man declaring the word of God daily, and he met his wife nine months later. William accepted an invitation to a BBQ, with people he barely knew, and almost a two-hour drive. The invitation included a mention of the possibility of a certain lovely blonde who might also attend the BBQ. The rest is history. (Almost. I did need to encourage William to send her a note via Facebook, and take her on a date.)

Pastor Kris Vallotton, in his message called "Hope, the Divine X-Factor" says this:

> **What do I do when I feel hopeless about a situation? I pretend it is not happening and ignore it; I don't do anything with it. "This I recall to my mind, therefore I have hope" (Lamentations 3:21).**
>
> **"I remember what God did for me" is a prophetic declaration about what He will do next time. Faith and hope and testimonies are a corporate garden. To have a testimony, you must go through the test. A testimony is when I have gone through a test and God came through.**
>
> **In Revelation it says the testimony of Jesus is the spirit of prophecy (see Revelation 29:11). Therefore, whatever He did for you, He will do for me, because God is no respecter of persons. So I can remember what God did for me, or I can take what God did for you and take it as a prophecy for me.**
>
> **It is history for you, and it is prophecy for me.**[1]

Allow the testimony of William and Megan to give you hope for today. I don't know the details of Megan's story, but I watched and prayed as God pulled William up from a desperate, desolate place, restored his career, and brought his wife to him. Their testimony, and the other testimonies of the marriages around us, are a prophecy for *you*! Are you in the test? God will come through for you *and* the person He has chosen as your marriage partner. Remember, the other person is in the test right now too, so pray for your future spouse as William and Megan prayed for each other years before they ever met.

Their story is also a testimony to accepting invitations to social events—you never know who you will meet.

DAY 6

One of the most poignant things I noticed about William and Megan's wedding was the way their Messianic Jewish pastor said, "I *declare* them, man and wife." I believe He carefully chose his words, knowing the power of a declaration.

Declarations:

1. We declare the God of our hope so fills each of us with all joy and peace in believing (through the experience of our faith) that by the power of the Holy Spirit we may abound and be overflowing (bubbling over) with hope! (See Romans 15:13 AMP.)
2. We declare we still dare to hope when we remember this: *The faithful love of the Lord never ends! His mercies never cease. Great is his faithfulness. His mercies begin afresh each morning.* (See Lamentations 3:21-23 NLT.)
3. I say to myself, "The Lord is my inheritance; therefore, I will *hope in Him!*"
4. The Lord is good to those who wait for Him, to the soul who seeks Him. It is good that I should hope and wait quietly for the salvation of the Lord! (See Lamentations 3:24-25.)
5. We declare as "David strengthened himself with trust in his God," we choose to strengthen and encourage ourselves, and we have hope, the divine X factor! (See 1 Samuel 30:6.)
6. We declare the testimonies of the marriages arranged by God in the lives of our family and friends are a prophecy of marriage for us and for all the people for whom we are praying. It is God's good and pleasing will that I am married.
7. Houses and riches are the inheritance from fathers, but a wise, understanding, and prudent wife is from the Lord. (See Proverbs 19:14.)

Amen! Expect to be amazed!

Day 7
Mountains of Separation

Summer in the Colorado Rockies is glorious! I love to escape the heat, head to the mountains, and set out on a long hike with my faithful Labrador, Schuyler. Perhaps because my mother often sang, "Raindrops on roses, and whiskers on kittens..." when we skied together, my mountain adventures often remind me of the Sound of Music, and my mother. (If I could only fit into my lederhosen from 8th grade.)

At the peak of summer in the Rockies, the mountainsides burst with color and life, and if you listen with your eyes, you can hear the flowers sing! The hills are alive with the sound of music!

It is on those mountain adventures I experience the most powerful prayer times, and a verse I have been declaring like a joyful song for a few years over my future husband is Song of Solomon 2:17:

> **Until the day breaks**
>
> **And the shadows flee away,**
>
> **Turn, my beloved, and be like a gazelle**
>
> **Or a young stag**
>
> **Upon the mountains of Bether.**

Why do I pray that verse? The Hebrew word Bether means *separation*—the mountains of separation! Are there mountains in your life blocking you from walking in the fullness of your destiny? What are the mountains of separation preventing marriage relationships? Are there obstacles you cannot see hindering you from meeting the person God has for you?

In his book *Faith and Confession,* Charles Capps describes "grace" as "God's willingness." This is what he says regarding Mark 11:23 (*...whoever says to this mountain, 'be removed…'*):

> Jesus is talking about problem areas in your life, about situations that you face and circumstances you don't know how to handle. He tells you to say to that situation, "Be plucked up, be planted in the sea; depart, be gone." Tell it what to do and where to go![1]
>
> This is the word of the Lord to Zerubbabel: "*Not by might nor by power, but by My Spirit,*" Says the LORD of hosts. "*Who are you, O Great Mountain? Before Zerubbabel you shall become a plain! And he shall bring forth the capstone* [Jesus] *With shouts of 'Grace, grace to it!'*"
>
> (Zechariah 4:6-7)

Imagine yourself on top of a mountain after a long hike with God's glory surrounding you and let's declare with authority!

Declarations:

Thank you, Father God, for this journey of faith; for Your faithfulness to lead us, and to instruct us in the power of Your spoken Word. "*Faith comes by hearing, and hearing by [speaking] the Word of God*" (Romans 10:17AMP). Fill our words with the power of Your Holy Spirit, and demolish the mountains of separation in our lives, and the lives of the men and women called to be our husbands and wives.

1. We declare that God's way is perfect; The Word of the Lord is proven; He is a shield to all who trust in Him. (See 2 Samuel 22:31.)
2. We declare that it is not by our might, nor by our power, but by the power of the Holy Spirit to break through in our lives, and the lives of the men and women called to marriage. (See Zechariah 4:6.)

3. We declare that we have faith in God, and we do not doubt. We speak to the mountains in our lives, with the authority of the King of kings—be plucked up, be planted in the sea; depart, be gone! (See Mark 11:23.)
4. We shout "Grace! Grace!" to the mountains of _____ (fill in the blank as things come to your mind: Separation, unbelief, disappointments, despair, rejection...). Depart! Be gone! (See Zechariah 4:7.)
5. We declare to our beloveds—come to us hastily. Be like a gazelle, or a young stag, and *leap* over the mountains that separate us. (See Song of Solomon 2:17.) We declare over ourselves and the people God has appointed as our spouses:

> God is our strength and power,
>
> And He makes our way perfect,
>
> He makes our feet like the feet of deer,
>
> And sets us on the high places.
>
> He teaches our hands to make war,
>
> So our arms can bend a bow of bronze,
>
> You have also given us the shield of Your salvation;
>
> Your gentleness has made us great.
>
> You enlarged our paths under us;
>
> So our feet do not slip.
>
> (See 2 Samuel 22:33-37.)

6. Thank you Father for bringing Your good gifts into our lives, and for exposing everything and anything that is an obstacle on the path of our destinies for good relationships and marriage.

Amen! Expect to be amazed!

Day 8
Wisdom and the Tree of Life

Inside my head there lives a dream that I want to see in the sun

Behind my eyes there lives a me that I've been hiding for much too long

I've gotta step out on faith, It's time to show my face

Procrastination had me down but look what I have found, I found

[Chorus:]

Strength, courage, and wisdom

And it's been inside of me all along,

Strength, courage, and wisdom

It's been inside of me all along, every day I'm praying for:

Strength, courage, and wisdom....

India Arie[1]

"Hope Deferred Makes the Heart Sick..."

Another party without a date or a friend to join me... "but I can do this! I know people there, it will be fun!"

Greeted by several friendly faces as I walked into the event, I anticipated a wonderful, festive evening. Alone, I stepped into the seafood buffet line so I would not miss the beautiful, fresh Alaskan fish that was disappearing quickly. My "datelessness" was bugging me as I stood in line with several couples for dinner.

Dinner is meant for community.

I filled my plate, and then I needed to find a place to sit and a group to join. I began praying, asking God to lead me to a table of welcoming friends with whom I could enjoy the lovely evening. I spotted a table of friends with empty chairs. Whew. Confidently, I asked if I could join them.

"Oh, so sorry, we have two more couples joining our table."

It was a table of couples, and there was no room for a solo diner. Ugh!

I began to feel disillusioned, and so alone among all those people. I couldn't even find my parents who were sitting with their friends. I quickly turned and walked through the party, surprised that the "friendly" place to sit was not as easy to find as I had hoped and prayed for.

Some people would say I "shouldn't" feel uncomfortable as a single person in a sea of couples; that I should be content in all things.

Content? Yes, I would say I was content. I *am* content. But that does not deny the pangs of longing for my companion—someone I could take to a social occasion—someone who would share my life.

Soon a friendly face waved me to his table, offering a seat and dining companions. It was the assurance that God was with me. He had a plan and I just needed to trust Him.

You may be more familiar with this verse than you would like: "Hope deferred makes the heart sick...." (Proverbs 13:12).

The Message puts it this way: "Unrelenting disappointment leaves you heartsick...."

The word for "sick" in Hebrew is: Chalah (Strong's #2470)[2]- and it means "to be rubbed worn, hence to be weak, sick, afflicted, or to grieve."

Hope deferred is abrasive. It wears you down, and the fabric of your heart gets weaker, and sick. The temptation is to build thick, protective, impenetrable walls around our wounded hearts.

DAY 8

How does one continue to hope when year after year, date after date, rejection after rejection, hope wanes and yields to unrelenting disappointment?

> But when desire comes, (when your dreams come true at last) it is a Tree of Life! (See Proverbs 13:12.)

> The fruit of the righteous is a tree of life (Proverbs 11:30).

> A gentle tongue [with its healing power] is a tree of life (Proverbs 15:4 AMP).

> Wisdom is a Tree of Life to those who embrace her; happy are those who hold her tightly (Proverbs 3:18 NLT).

While we wait for the desire to come, let's ask the Lord for a Tree of Life. Seek wisdom from God to navigate the path ahead and to move forward into His best for your life. When you ask God for wisdom, He will give it to you in abundance!

> If any of you lacks wisdom, you should ask God, who gives generously to all without finding fault, and it will be given to you (James 1:5 NIV).

As we turn to Jesus and seek the hidden treasures of wisdom, our weakened hearts will become happy, healthy and strong. It is wise to speak kind and gentle words with a tongue full of healing power.

When desire comes, when your dreams come true, it is a Tree of Life, and the leaves of the Tree of Life are for the healing of the nations. Marriage brings forth life. When two people commit to love, honor, respect, and encourage each other, pray together, and love God together, there is healing in the world around them. One of the aspects of the healing of nations is a multitude of healthy marriages. So may the fruit of your life and your future marriage be a Tree of Life to the world around you.

Declarations

Thank you, Father God, that with You, *all* things are possible. With You, there is always a *but!* *But* when desire comes...*but* God! Thank you for giving us hope, healing, restoration, and happiness; and thank you for Your faithfulness to fulfill Your promises. Thank you for Your "strength, courage, and wisdom."

1. For all the men and women praying for their marriage, we declare Colossians 2:2-3. That our hearts may be encouraged, knit together in love, attaining to all riches of understanding, the mystery of God, in whom are hidden **all the treasures of wisdom** and knowledge. (Selah—meditate and say it again.)
2. We know when we ask for wisdom, God gives us this gift generously, without holding back. (See James 1:5.) We thank God for His wisdom, and declare that we are receiving an increase of wisdom.
3. Wisdom is the Tree of Life to those who embrace her, and we are called happy because we embrace wisdom tightly. (See Proverbs 3:18.)
4. We pray to the God of our Lord Jesus Christ, the Father of Glory that He may grant us a spirit of wisdom and revelation in the knowledge of Him. (See Ephesians 1:17 AMP.)
5. As we commit our way to the Lord, and trust in Him, He will bring forth our righteousness as the light, and justice as the noonday. The fruit of the righteous is a Tree of Life! (See Psalm 37:5-6 and Proverbs 11:30.)
6. We declare we have a gentle and kind tongue that speaks words of life and healing; and it is a tree of life. (See Proverbs 15:4.)
7. We choose to rest in the Lord and we wait patiently for Him. (See Psalm 37:7.)

Amen! Expect to be amazed!

Day 9
Divine Alliances

It has been my observation that divorce is never without excruciating pain for everyone involved. One of the Hebrew definitions for the word divorce is a "cutting off from marriage." I have also witnessed marriages ending too soon through the more devastatingly painful experience of losing a spouse to death. I cannot fathom the loss and heartache.

In both cases, the people involved are left alone after knowing the oneness of marriage. One of the first things God said as recorded in the Bible was, *"It is not good for man* (or woman) *to be alone"* (see Genesis 2:18). The Hebrew word for alone, which has been mentioned before, is "bad" from the root word *badad*, which means "To disjoin, to divide, to separate. The notion of cutting or tearing apart, and hence of dividing..."[1] Strong's concordance, #H909.

That word, "bad," has another definition, which is "apart from." Apart from what? Apart from the whole; from the union of man and wife?

The older you are in your dating life, the more likely you are to meet people who were previously married. Many have experienced the pain of loss at a deeper level than those of us who have not married. We have all experienced some loss or rejection, *but God* is bringing restoration. It all seems messy at times, but let me encourage you with an excerpt from a book called *Divine Alliances* by Doug Addison:

> **"A divine realignment will occur that brings couples together for the strategic purpose of God's Kingdom. Suddenly many people who**

> were divorced or widowed will begin to remarry at an accelerated rate. Though divorce and death are not God's will, God will redeem them.
>
> God will bring great surprises as He repays people for the years of suffering they have experienced.
>
> Those who focus on God will not miss His new purposes.
>
> A word about divorce: The divine alliances that God showed me were between people who had gone through a lot of difficult times before they met each other. Some had battled to stay married, then had gone through divorce and God had brought a new spouse; still others were widowed, having lost their spouse through death. I saw God begin to bring together these types of people as couples who would have a single focus and a purpose of expanding God's Kingdom.
>
> I want to clarify that God is the one who is orchestrating divine alliances." Doug Addison[2]

When I think about the redemption of God for those who have experienced divorce, the words I keep hearing in my mind are, "repairer of the breach." In Old Testament Israel, a breach was a gap or breakdown in a wall or protection surrounding a city, allowing the enemy to come in to steal, kill, and destroy. I believe that many who have been through the destruction of divorce or the loss of a spouse will be instruments of God's restoration in the lives of others. Rebuilding the walls of marriage will strengthen society as a whole.

> I will always show you where to go. I'll give you a full life in the emptiest of places; firm muscles, strong bones. You'll be like a well-watered garden, a gurgling spring that never runs dry. You'll use the old rubble of past lives to build anew, rebuild the foundations from out of your past.
>
> You'll be known as those who can fix anything, restore old ruins, rebuild and renovate, make the community livable again (Isaiah 58:11-12 MSG).

DAY 9

Declarations:

Thank you Father God that You are a God of Restoration! Thank you for speaking through Doug Addison, and we come into agreement with his revelations for our lives.

1. We agree and declare God is orchestrating divine alliances, and bringing couples together for the strategic purpose of God's Kingdom.
2. We declare the "suddenlies" of God—that many people who were divorced, widowed, or not yet married will begin to marry and remarry at an accelerated rate.
3. Thank you, Lord, for surprises, and we declare that You are repaying and restoring us from the years of suffering and what we see as the loss of time. The Lord is redeeming the time.
4. We choose to focus on God, and we will not miss His new purposes.
5. From Isaiah 58:11 (MSG), we declare "God will always show us the way we are to go. He will give us a full life in the emptiest of places. He is giving us firm muscles and strong bones. We are like a well-watered garden, and a gurgling spring that never runs dry, because His Holy Spirit dwells in us."
6. We declare God is using the old rubble of our past lives to build anew, and rebuild and restore from the past.
7. We are called "repairer of the breach!" By Your Spirit, Lord, we declare those of us who have been torn apart by divorce or loss of a love will be restored and united with the best companion. We call forth our divine alliances.

Amen! Expect to be amazed!

Day 10
True Beauty

The end of the relationship was rough, and then it became even more painful. A second kick in the gut came when I was already down, threatening to push me over the edge, deeper into the abyss of self-doubt and self-consciousness.

After four months of progressing into a "love" relationship, Sam told me the reason he ended our relationship was that he was no longer attracted to me physically. He suggested that at my age I could use a little plastic surgery, go on a diet, get in better shape. "Women your age re-beautify," he said, thinking he was helping me for my next relationship.

I was stunned, my jaw hit the ground, and then I laughed! "That is not insurmountable," I argued. "I can lose a few pounds."

His words were shocking after months of talking about our future together and imagining a ministry together. It seemed that God had a plan for us and we talked about His plan, prayed together, and at Sam's suggestion, read a book on marriage together.

Oh yeah, it gets worse. Sam's response, "No, I am not willing to wait around for you to lose weight. If it was going to take three days, maybe, but it's going to take you a long time."

"What? Did he really just say that?!"

When I realized the shallow words were coming out of the mouth of a man I thought could be my husband, I told him he needed to get out of my house. He *flew* out the door.

DAY 10

Ladies, I have nothing against plastic surgery and "re-beautifying." And I have entertained thoughts of improving my physique. But extra nips, tucks and lifts are a luxury, and after many skin cancer surgeries, I was not interested in knives and needles. Getting in better condition was very doable, and something I planned on doing anyway. I already had a healthy lifestyle.

But more importantly, we need to remember true beauty shines from the inside out.

Just to give you an accurate picture, seven weeks earlier we hiked the highest peak in Colorado, Mt. Elbert, and it had the potential of being a romantic adventure. He was behind me most of the way up, encouraging me with cheers of, "we can *do* this!" I thought it was such a beautiful picture of relationship. We did make it to the top of the mountain, and it was excruciating and exhilarating—to the point of tears.

Little did I know the "perfect storm" was right around the corner. So maybe I had gained a few pounds, as we do, but my clothes still fit fine. Sam began dropping hints about what I was eating, and he made suggestions on working out together, but I didn't think much of what he was saying. I am glad I paid no attention to his not-so-subtle hints, because my temporary weight gain caused his shallow, ugly person to emerge.

The assault was on my appearance and attractiveness, and I must share with you that I was so thankful for the book, *Captivating*, in the days following. As John and Stasi Eldredge explain in the book, the enemy, our enemy, has an extra measure of hatred towards women and particularly our beauty. We women have the unique gift from God to offer beauty to the world, and our true beauty is the target of the enemy's attacks.

Beauty is the essence of a woman. Every little girl (and big girl) is asking one fundamental question. Little girls want to know, "am I lovely?" [1]

They go on to explain that both physical beauty and inner beauty are the essence of a woman, and they are integrated – "one depends on and flows out of the other." Our culture is focused on the perfect look and physique, a standard we compare ourselves to, only to see all of our imperfections.

If you have not read *Captivating*, I recommend it to both men and women. I read it years ago, but returned to the book soon after being told I was unacceptable and not lovely. John and Stasi Eldredge bring clarity to our struggles as women, revealing that we do have an enemy in the story of our lives. We have been wounded, *but God* is the God who heals and restores our hearts. He is the God of hope! Read on.

> **Renounce the agreements you've made. Your wounds brought messages with them. Lots of messages. Somehow they all usually landed in the same place. They had a familiar theme. "You're worthless." "You're not a woman." "You're too much…and not enough." "you're a disappointment." "You are repulsive." On and on they go. Because they were delivered with such pain, they felt true. They pierced our hearts, and they seemed so true. So we accepted the message as fact. We embraced it as the verdict on us.**[2]

Many times the repeated issues and struggles we face are rooted in the vows we made as children. We made agreements with the wounding messages and those vows will direct our steps away from God's best, and into unhealthy patterns until we renounce and reject them. My friend, Tim, was told he would never measure up as a man by his wife of 17 years. She made a vow as a child that she would never be married to a "poor" man. So when they went through financial struggles, she had two affairs trying to find that guy who would not be poor in her eyes. The marriage ended, and the children suffered the most because of the strength of her childhood vow.

The Eldredges continue:

> **We must reject the message of our wounds. It's a way of unlocking the door to Jesus. Agreements lock the door from the inside. Renouncing the agreements unlocks the door to Him.**[3]

Declarations

1. Thank you Lord for the power of Your forgiveness. Forgive me for receiving the lies as truth, and for any vows I have made. I renounce

DAY 10

the vows and agreements of _____ (take time to listen to your heart). You say that I am a son/daughter of the King of kings. I am loved and worthy.
2. And thank you Spirit of Truth for continuing to reveal the lies as we speak the powerful truth of God's Word and His promises.
3. My King desires my beauty; I am fearfully and wonderfully made; I am the apple of God's eye! (See Psalm 45:11, Psalm 139:14, and Psalm 17:8.)
4. We declare we are a crown of beauty in the hand of the Lord, and a royal diadem in the hand of our God. (See Isaiah 62:3 AMP.)
5. We declare that with God nothing is ever impossible and no word from God shall be without power or impossible of fulfillment. (See Luke 1:37 AMP.)
6. I declare that I am God's creation, and I am altogether lovely and my beloved (to be) is altogether lovely. (See Song of Solomon 1:5, and 5:16.)
7. We declare that we are anxious for nothing. The peace of God, which surpasses all understanding, is guarding our hearts and minds through Christ Jesus. We choose to meditate on things that are noble, just, pure, lovely, and are of good report. (See Philippians 4:6-8.)

Go back and say these again. Let them take root in your heart and continue to declare the truth of who you are:

A daughter or son of the King!

Every man or woman wants in their spouse a person who knows who he or she is.

Amen! Expect to be amazed!

Day 11
Delight to Desire

My sister Lisa often has great nuggets of wisdom to share with me, as she did the day before her only son's wedding. We were talking about trusting God and His perfect plan, even when it does not make sense. And I am sure the conversation was related to my life and my wait in meeting Mr. Right. Lisa is wise, and her nugget was full of double wisdom because she was quoting the brilliant King David. *"Delight yourself also in the Lord, and He shall give you the desires of your heart"* (Psalm 37:4).

Later that day, I read an email that contained a message titled, "Desires and Dreams of the Heart" by Garris Elkins—an inspired message on the same verse. I have learned to pay attention when I hear the same verse from two different sources, two or more times in a day, so I will share a snippet with you here:

> **When we were made one with God through Jesus Christ, the very desires of our heart had the potential to reflect the same desires that reside in God's heart. This is possible because the Holy Spirit—God—lives within us.**[1]

Your desire to meet your life companion and for a glorious marriage comes straight from the heart of God! It is a good desire, so keep it alive.

> **Delight yourself in the Lord, and He will give you the desires and secret petitions of your heart (Psalm 37:4 AMP).**

DAY 11

Hope deferred makes the heart sick, but

...when desire comes, it is the tree of life (Proverbs 13:12).

When you hear "delight yourself in the Lord," what does that mean to you? The definition I have known is to *take pleasure in, delight in...as in the Hebrew word, chaphets,* Strong's #2654. I must admit, I don't always feel like "delighting" myself in the Lord, *especially* when I am in a place of hope deferred. Feeling the weight of discouragement convincing me to let go of my lifeline of hope.

When looking up the word "delight," I was surprised to learn the word in Psalm 37:4 means to be soft and delicate. It also means a woman enticing or inviting a man into romance, so we are to delight in or "woo" God, and enjoy our relationship with Him.

Job 22 says that as we acquaint ourselves with the Lord, return to Him, and receive instruction from Him. Then we will have our *delight* in the Almighty; He will hear our prayers, and when we declare a thing, it will be established!

For me, the weddings of my family members, a generation younger than I, were always an opportunity for me to delve into self-pity, wondering why I was not taking a turn on the wedding circuit. On that day of my nephew's wedding, as on the day of many other weddings, I needed a focus shift. Changing from my lack, to choosing to see and enjoy what God was doing, and bubble over with delight in Him.

> **You'll take delight in God, the Mighty One, and look to him joyfully, boldly. You'll pray to him and he'll listen; he'll help you do what you've promised. You'll decide what you want and it will happen; your life will be bathed in light (Job 22:26-28 MSG).**

Delighting yourself in the Lord is having a posture of gladness, happiness, contentment, and wooing – focused on Him. When your focus is on the fun you are having with God, you will not be desperate and bleak. You will be more attractive to the one God is bringing into your life.

Declarations

Thank you, Almighty God, for Your Word today. Thank you for reassuring us that as we declare Your Word, it will be established for Your purposes, in Your perfect time. Thank you for Your promise that when we delight ourselves in the Lord, You will give us the desires and secret petitions of our hearts.

1. We commit everything we do to the Lord. We trust Him, and He will help us. He will make our innocence radiate like the dawn, and the justice of our cause will shine like the noonday sun. (See Psalm 37:5-6 NLV.)
2. We declare our heart's desire is to be acquainted with You, our Lord; that we will be at peace, and *good* will come to us! (See Job 22:21.)
3. We declare we are open to receive Your instruction, and we lay up Your words in our hearts. (See Job 22:22.)
4. Impart to us the will to return to You, God Almighty, for Your restoration, and shine Your light on anything hidden in our lives. Now give us strength to release it all to You for Your cleansing and healing. (See Job 22:23.)
5. We declare the desire for marriage is restored in the hearts of the men and women called to unite in marriage.
6. We have delight in You, the Almighty, and we lift our faces to You, God. (See Job 22:26.)
7. Thank you, Lord, that You are faithful to hear our deep desires and fulfill the secret petitions of our hearts, because we are soft and pliable; focused on Your beautiful face.

Amen! Expect to be amazed!

Day 12
From Jealousy to Celebration

When a dear friend pointed out to me the frustration I had been feeling might be jealousy and covetousness, I knew she was right. It was subtle, and I was not even conscious that I was coveting. Perhaps I was a little bit jealous of the new bride Angie's amazing love story. That's what friends are for—to point out to us what we cannot see.

In a conversation, I was expressing my frustration with Angie and some of her pre-wedding requests, but deep down I was harboring disappointment that I was not the one experiencing the incredible and sudden romance. It was one of those *God—why her and not me* moments. I was becoming irritated when she would say, "I have been waiting sooooo long for my husband." The sense of entitlement came upon me. I was 13 years older, so my wait was much longer for reasons I will never know or understand.

When we hear the testimony of how God is moving in the lives of other people in the area of marriage, it is meant to encourage us because it is a demonstration of God's goodness and faithfulness. As we said in chapter 6, the testimonies of other people can be taken as a prophecy for us if we celebrate what God is doing in the lives of our friends. But beware of the trap of jealousy.

In the Old Testament, there are several examples of the spirit of jealousy coming upon people. It brings anger and, I will add, frustration and resentment.

> **Jealousy is as cruel (severe) as the grave; its flames are flames of fire, a most vehement flame (Song of Solomon 8:6).**

When the true colors of my heart were pointed out to me, I spent time repenting and declared the doors of jealousy and covetousness closed! So I pose the question to you today:

Do you feel the rustling of frustration or self-pity when you hear that God is bringing other people together in marriage or relationships?

Ask God to show you anywhere you may have opened the door to the spirit of jealousy. Repent, and rejoice for the goodness of God in the lives of your friends. Speak a blessing over your friends and their marriages.

Remember: *"Rejoice with those who rejoice"* (Romans 12:15).

Declarations

God, we declare You are good! We *"taste and see the Lord is good! And blessed is the man who trusts in Him!"* (See Psalm 34:8.)

1. Father God, forgive me for cooperating with the spirit of jealousy in my life. I bless my friends and family who found love, prosperity, and anything else my heart is aching and waiting for.
2. We waited patiently for the Lord to help us; He turned to us, and heard our cries! He lifted us out of the pit of despair.... (See Psalm 40:1-2 NLT.)
3. Thank you for "the *joy* of those who trust the Lord." We declare our trust in You, Lord. (See Psalm 40:4 NLT.)
4. It is *good* to give thanks to the Lord and to sing praise to Your name, O Most high. We declare Your loving-kindness in the morning, and Your faithfulness every night! For You, Lord, have made us glad through Your work; we will triumph in the works of Your hands. (See Psalm 92:1-5.)
5. I will sing of the Lord's great love forever; with my mouth I will make Your faithfulness known through all generations. I will declare that Your love stands firm forever, that you have established Your faithfulness in heaven itself. (See Psalm 89:1 NIV.)
6. We declare that we will see the goodness of the Lord in the land of the living. (What would have become of me) had I not believed that

DAY 12

I would see the Lord's goodness in the land of the living? (See Psalm 27:13 AMP.)
7. We declare that we wait and hope for and expect the Lord; we are brave and of good courage and we let our hearts be stout and enduring. Yes, we wait for and hope for and expect the Lord. (See Psalm 27:14 AMP.)

Amen! Expect to be amazed!

Day 13
Invest in New Wineskins

It is no secret I enjoy good wine, and love exploring the craft and romance in the wine regions of the world. One of my favorite wines comes from the Stag's Leap area of Napa Valley, California, known for some of the best Cabernets in the world. One of my favorite prayers for my future husband is for him to "be like a stag and leap over the mountains that separate us!" (See Day 7 and Song of Solomon 2:13.) Because of the verse, I had a great bottle of Stag's Leap wine that I was saving, with a vision of a special dinner with the man God is bringing into my life.

However, that particular bottle came off the shelf the day I said farewell to my beloved Labrador, Samson. For 13 years he had been by my side as we hiked and prayed and declared many scriptures, including the Song of Solomon verse above. Samson, an athletic dog, even had a bounding run and leap much like that of a stag. It was the perfect bottle of wine to drink in celebration of my wonderful stag-like-leaping dog. I thanked God daily for the gift of Samson; an extraordinary, faithful, joy-filled companion during some challenging years of singleness.

You have experienced the cycles of hope and disappointment, and perhaps had the thoughts or feelings that if you temper your hope, then you will not be as disappointed if things don't work out. The cycles enlarge and shrink our hearts, like an expanding and emptying wineskin. After the hope and "hope deferreds" of life, your heart becomes dry and brittle like an old wineskin unable to receive and contain new, fresh, vibrant wine.

> **And no one puts new wine into old wineskins; or else the new wine bursts the wineskins, the wine is spilled and the wineskins**

DAY 13

are ruined. But new wine must be put into new wineskins (Mark 2:22).

The old wineskins represent our hearts in past relationships containing the love given and received. You may have had fine wine, rare and irreplaceable, or good wine, or not-so-good wine, but...take heart!

New wine is coming! Be expectant! And get ready!

> Hope is a divine force based in the confidence that He is good and that He intends to do good things in us, for us, and through us—today, tomorrow, this month, this year, and in the days to come. Bob Hartley[1]

We are preparing for God's best for a new marriage, and we need a fresh, clean heart to contain new love. When new wine is poured into the wineskins, it expands, which is the reason for a new wineskin. We need soft, supple, forgiving hearts—free from the past. A result of delighting ourselves in the Lord (see Day 11).

Offer your old brittle wineskin, your past and loves lost, to the Lord, and allow Him to do His transformational work. Your heart will be able to contain the new love that will bless and expand your life.

> God, your God, will cut away the thick calluses on your heart... freeing you to love God, your God, with your whole heart and soul, and live, really live! (Deuteronomy 30:6-7 MSG).

> And you shall return and obey the voice of the Lord and do all His commandments which I command you today. And the Lord your God will make you abundantly prosperous in every work of your hand, in the fruit of your body, of your cattle, of your land, for good; for the Lord will again delight in prospering you, as He took delight in your fathers (Deuteronomy 30:8-9 AMP).

> And the Lord your God will bring much good upon all the work you do, and upon your children, and the young of your cattle, and the food

of your field. For the Lord will again be happy to bring good to you, just as He was happy with your fathers (Deuteronomy 30:9 NLV).

Declarations

Father God, we come to You today to ask for a transformation of our hearts and the hearts of other men and women called to Kingdom marriages. Replace the old, brittle wineskins, and use Your loving scalpel to do a good work on our hearts. We have a past full of disappointments, hope deferred, love that faded, heartbreak, and images of our ideal spouse, but we place it on Your operating table—the altar. We repent and lay down any blame we put on God that might be hidden.

1. We declare God is good! And He intends to do good things in our lives. God is in favor of our desire for marriage. "Every good and perfect gift is from above, coming down from the Father of the heavenly lights who does not change like shifting shadows." (See James 1:17 NIV.)
2. We declare our hearts are being circumcised by Your Holy Spirit. Cut away the calluses of our past and demolish the unhealthy walls around our hearts.
3. We declare all old wineskins of the heart, and the appetite for the old wine (relationships, and the image of the ideal or idols) are handed over to You, Lord, for Your transformational work. We agree with Isaiah 43:18, and declare the Lord is doing a *new* thing! We choose "not to remember the former things; nor consider the things of old."
4. Fill our hearts with fresh love for You, Lord, our first love; and we declare that we will love You with all of our mind and heart and with all of our being, that we may live. (See Deuteronomy 30:6 AMP.)
5. We declare life over areas of the hearts that are calloused, dry, withering, or shrinking from disappointments. Supernaturally defibrillate our hearts today.
6. We receive the *new* wine skins. And we declare the new wine, the new, expanding love, is coming!
7. Thank you that Your Word promises as we love You and follow Your commandments, You will abundantly prosper the work of our hands, and

the fruit of our bodies. Thank you, Lord, that You delight in prospering Your children!

I love You Lord, my God.

Cheers to the new wine!

Amen! Expect to be amazed!

Day 14
A New View of Trials

My brethren, count it all joy, when you fall into various trials, knowing the testing of your faith produces patience. But let patience have its perfect (mature) work, that you may be perfect and complete, lacking nothing (James 1:2).

I thought that verse meant that I should be happy about the trial in the midst of my suffering, thanking God for everything, when my emotions are the opposite. Just put on a happy face and pretend that I'm OK. How long can we keep up the false front before it crumbles into a bigger mess?

One day I was washing dishes with the radio tuned to Dr. Jeremiah teaching about James 1:2—and his insights captured my attention. I heard him say that "count it all joy" does not mean we are thankful for the trial, or that we must pretend it's fun. It means that we see how God is going to use the trial in our lives, and we can be joyful as we imagine the outcome and the victory.

I looked up the phrase "count it" from James 1:2 in *Strong's* #G2233, and this is what I found:

1. To lead:
    a) To go before;
    b) To be a leader;
    c) To rule, command.
2. To have authority over.
3. A prince, of regal power, governor, viceroy, chief, leading as respects influence, controlling in counsel, overseers or leaders of the churches.

4. Used of any kind of leader, chief, commander.
5. The leader in speech, chief, spokesman.
6. To consider, deem, account, think.

So, my interpretation changed. I began to see that when we go through the storms and various trials, we are to envision the future, the victory, the marriage. We then lead, and take authority over the discouragement and disappointment attempting to keep us crushed, ineffective, unattractive, and not available.

After my new understanding of "count it all joy," I went for my daily prayer walk. I imagined myself full of real joy with a godly man. I thanked God for that which is to come. I am *choosing* to walk through the challenges of today with joy, knowing that the future vision is getting closer every day.

> **For you know that when your faith is tested, your endurance has a chance to grow. So let it grow, for when your endurance is fully developed, you will be perfect and complete, needing nothing (James 1:3-4 NLV).**
>
> **If any of you lacks wisdom, let him ask of God, who gives to all liberally and without reproach, and it will be given to him (James 1:5).**

Jesus endured the betrayal, abuse, and ultimate death on the cross because He saw the joy set before Him! And He *despised* the shame. (See Hebrews 12:2.)

I will leave you with the definition of the word "endures" from the notes in my bible:

Endures, *hupomeno*; Strong's #5278: To hold one's ground in conflict, bear up against adversity, hold out under stress, stand firm, persevere under pressure, wait calmly and courageously. It is not passive resignation to fate and mere patience, but the active, energetic resistance to defeat that allows calm and brave endurance.[1]

Declarations

Thank you, Heavenly Father, for Your faithfulness, and for walking beside us every step of the way. Thank you that You have a plan for our lives, to prosper us and not to harm us, to give us a future and a hope. (See Jeremiah 29:11.)

1. We declare that when we are in the storms and trials of life, we count it all joy, and we look to the victorious one, Jesus Christ. We *see* the victory and the fulfillment of God's promises in our lives. (Describe your vision out loud now—the more detail the better. Feel the emotion of victory.)
2. Thank you, Lord, that when our faith is tested, our endurance and patience is strengthened and matured. We declare that we are becoming stronger in patience and endurance, and we lack nothing!
3. We declare that we need wisdom, and we ask our generous Father God for His wisdom in our lives. He gives us wisdom liberally and without reproach or shame! (See James 1:5.)
4. We declare we have been given eyes to see the joy set before us, and we despise any shame that is trying to hold us back from our destinies and desires. (See Hebrews 12:2.)
5. We declare we have endurance. We have the strength and fortitude to "hold our ground in conflict, hold out under stress, stand firm and persevere under pressure. We wait calmly and courageously!" (*Strong's* definition of the word "endures.")
6. We take His joy as our strength to walk through the trials to the victory! (See Nehemiah 8:10.)
7. We declare that we will not lose heart, because we believe that we will see the goodness of the Lord in the land of the living. (See Psalm 27:13.)

Amen! Expect to be amazed!

Day 15
Marriage is a Mission

The point of marriage isn't marriage.

It's a picture.

A display.

A window that you look through to something else.

A marriage has a mission.

When we go to a wedding, maybe we're so moved because we want this new couple to succeed. We intuitively know that their "success" is somehow tied to ours. Their making of love makes the world a better place to live, a place where there is more love for all of us. Maybe this is why we always notice great marriages. When their love is growing, it inspires us. Their life together gives us life. Rob Bell[1]

During our inaugural "40 Days of Declarations," when 30 people were praying for 40 days and declaring God's truth for marriage, several people met their future spouse, and a few weddings were scheduled!

One holy union was indeed a marriage with a mission. I was privileged to witness the exchanging of vows of Sylvia and Steve. As I watched and listened to the ceremony, it was clear the joining of Sylvia and Steve was designed by God for His divine purposes. Not only is their marriage now a blessing for each of them individually, but they have a mission to fulfill together they cannot accomplish apart. Sylvia and Steve pressed through obstacles and naysayers, and they told the hindering mountains to move, trusting that God had brought them together for such a time as this.

Friends and family blessed the couple, and I was sincerely rejoicing for them and with them. Yet I must honestly and humbly admit to the tension between the joy I felt for this marriage, and the pang in my heart from a recent break-up. Then I saw two of my dear unmarried prayer warrior friends near the front, and wondered if they were feeling the same tension. These are normal feelings. In times like these I am learning to take captive those thoughts and instead rejoice with those who are rejoicing. Resting in the truth that my time is coming.

When you celebrate the good stuff that happens to others, you are positioning yourself to receive the good stuff God wants to do for you. Rejoice with those who rejoice! Bob Hazlett[2]

Choose to *believe* our prayers are effective! We are moving the mountains that are standing between people who are aching to meet their marriage partner!

Declarations

Thank you, dear Lord, for fresh hope. Thank you for the marriages and weddings soon to come among our family and friends. Bless them, Lord, with Your gifts of romance and love. We want them to succeed and, as their love is multiplied, let more love be dispersed into our communities. The success of others is our success too.

1. Lord, You have a much larger purpose in these marriages, and You have given us the desire in our hearts for marriage. We declare that we delight ourselves in the Lord, and He will give us the desires of our hearts.
2. We declare the joy of the Lord is our strength, and we choose to hope and believe God is directing our steps each day closer to the person He has chosen for us. (See Nehemiah 8:11 and Psalm 119:133.)
3. This is the word of the Lord to us: "Not by might nor by power, but by My Spirit Says the Lord of hosts." Who are you, oh great mountain? Before us you shall become a plain! We shout "grace, grace" to the mountains hindering marriages! (See Zechariah 4:6-7.)

4. We declare that marriage is God's good plan for His people. We declare that no weapon formed against those of us who are called to marriage will prosper. (See Isaiah 54:17.)
5. Thank you Lord God that with You nothing is impossible—nothing! Thank you that You, Jesus, have instructed us to speak to all mountains of separation, "Be plucked up, be planted in the sea; depart, be gone!" (See Mark 11:23.)
6. Thank you Lord that You raise up the men called to Kingdom marriage. Give them the attributes of Boaz: the strength and wisdom of a warrior; prosperity, kindness, favor in the community; and the ability to redeem and restore. (See Ruth 2:1-2.)
7. And as women, we declare towards the men chosen by God for our marriage with a mission, "Let me find favor in Your sight…" and the men will take God's best women under their wing. (See Ruth 3:9.)[3]

Amen! Expect to be amazed!

Day 16
The Woman Will Encompass the Man

Early in my experience of reading the Bible, the Lord highlighted a verse, penetrating my heart and spirit. I believe it is rich with wisdom for women seeking a Godly marriage. The moment I read it, I knew part of my role as a wife would be to surround and protect my husband with my prayers and encouraging words. At the time I was not married, but the truths I discovered extended to other men in my life—my father, my pastor, and my boss.

Many of the commentators have been confused by this mysterious verse, so as my friend Ed Silvoso would say, "Let the Holy Spirit speak to you." I pray you have the spirit of wisdom and revelation as you read and pray.

> **How long will you gad about, O you backsliding daughter?**
>
> *For the LORD has created a new thing in the earth A woman shall encompass a man* (Jeremiah 31:22).
>
> **How long will you wander, unfaithful (or faithless) Daughter Israel?**
>
> *The LORD will create a new thing on the earth – the woman will return to* (will protect) *the man* (Jeremiah 31:22 NIV).

The word "man" in the verse above is one of four words for "man" in the Old Testament.

Man, *geber;* **Strong's** #1397: A champion, hero, warrior, mighty man; a man in all his strength. This word describes a man of strength or bravery.[1]

I've had conversations with several men who deeply long to meet their wives—women who will encourage them to be all that God has called them to be as

DAY 16

mighty men. Some of the stories are heartbreaking of former wives who contributed to the destruction of their marriages. Their words emasculating their husbands, lashing with their tongues, causing shame, and knocking the men down from a place of strength to weakness. Words are powerful.

I believe our culture has helped damage the relationships between men and women through TV shows, magazines, and much of what we have accepted as "progress."

So what *does* it mean for a woman to encompass a man? The more I ponder this thought, the more I see ways in which women are designed to surround, protect, and encompass their husbands, and to respect the other men in their lives.

The human ribcage is strong, yet fragile, and designed to surround and protect the vital organs in the body, particularly the heart and lungs. Could it be that woman was intentionally fashioned and built by God from one of Adam's ribs as a sign of her purpose to encompass him?

*"The **heart** of her husband safely trusts her; so he will have no lack of gain"* (Proverbs 31:11). I think God is serious about this, ladies!

"An excellent wife is the crown of her husband, but she who causes shame is like rottenness in his bones" (Proverbs 12:4). A crown surrounds the head of a king, so we are to protect the mind of the men through our prayers and positive, respectful, encouraging words.

Did you hear that? *"But she who causes shame is like rottenness in his bones."* Can a man stand if he has rottenness in his bones? Women use criticism of men as an effort to gain control.

In some Jewish wedding ceremonies, "the tradition of the bride circling the groom is an allusion to the prophecy regarding the Messianic Era: 'The female will surround [and protect] the male.' With these circles, the bride is creating an invisible wall around her husband into which she will step—to the exclusion of all others." [2] What a beautiful illustration of a woman encompassing her man.

In the process of making declarations for marriages, I've had a new thought about what it means to encompass and protect a man. It comes from being grounded in our own faith, and not grasping at a man to fulfill our insecure needs. Quiet confidence in God provides a safe place for a man to be his vulnerable self. Sometimes they need a peaceful space to express their struggles. We can offer that space with no judgment and no demands when we are confident our identity and value come from God.

To the women: Ask God to transform you into a woman who loves and trusts God with all of your heart, soul, mind and strength. You are free to encompass the man He is bringing to you and able to create a safe place for him.

The assignment for the women:

1. Give words of encouragement and pray protection over the men.
2. Pray for men's hearts to be soft to the touch of Christ.
3. Pray for their lungs to remain filled with the life-giving breath of God.
4. Pray for protection over the men's minds; that God gives them wisdom and discernment; and that they have the mind of Christ—power, love, and a sound mind!

These are written for the women to say; so men, change these to declarations for the woman God has for you, and for other women called to marriage.

Declarations

Father, thank you for unwrapping Your Word for us with fresh revelation. Search our hearts and expose the lies we have accepted regarding how women are to relate to, respond to, and care for the hearts of the men in our lives.

1. Repent first: Return (turn and go the opposite direction). On behalf of the women we represent, who are longing for and called to marriages, we declare that we will return to Your Kingdom order in our relationships with men. Lord, shine Your light in our hearts and minds to reveal any area of our lives that needs Your healing and redemption. (Selah...meditate on this.)
2. We declare and agree that we will surround and protect men through prayer, encouragement, kind words, and peace; providing a space for them to share their lives with us.

3. We declare "I am a virtuous wife. The heart of my (future) husband safely trusts me; so he will have no lack of gain." (See Proverbs 31:11.)
4. We declare the words of our mouths, and the meditation of our hearts, are acceptable in Your sight, oh Lord, our strength and our Redeemer. (See Psalm 19:14.)
5. We declare we are called to be an excellent wife, a wife of valor, which is the crown of her husband. As a crown encircles and protects a man's head, we declare that we will surround and protect the man's mind and thoughts with a shield of prayer. (See Proverbs 12:4.)
6. We declare that our tongues are wholesome and healing, which is a Tree of Life. (See Proverbs 15:4.)
7. We declare that we will speak pleasant words that are like honeycomb; they are sweetness to the soul, and words that bring health to the bones. (See Proverbs 16:24.)

Amen! Expect to be amazed!

Day 17
Woo Him, and Uncover His Feet!

> For the Lord has created a new thing in the land [of Israel]; a female shall compass (woo, win and protect) a man (Jeremiah 31:22 AMP).

In the last chapter we focused on the translation of Jeremiah 31:22 that spoke of the woman protecting the man through prayer and encouraging words. Today we look at the word "compass" as the woman wooing or winning the man.

Ruth & Boaz

Take a look at Ruth chapter 3, because there are some keys for women who are seeking the "security or rest" of marriage. As I was reading the book of Ruth for this prayer project, for the first time, I saw Naomi as the Holy Spirit. The name Naomi means "delightful renewal."

Ruth left her hometown, and accompanied her mother in law, Naomi on a journey into the unknown. Ruth was committed and submitted to Naomi, trusting her enough to do the most risky and unconventional things.

Have you said, *"all that you say to me I will do"* to the Holy Spirit? It's His voice above all others we need to hear, trust, and obey on this journey. There are so many "rules" about dating, and guidelines are good to follow, but not to the exclusion of the still soft voice of the Holy Spirit. I have been diligent to follow the rules, and to relate to men according to books I read, or advice from friends. But books and friends are quick to fix you, or fix you up.

DAY 17

But God!

I love the message in Ruth because there was a time of waiting and a journey away from the comforts of the old season. Ruth chose to take her eyes and focus off her own circumstances after the death of her husband, to selflessly serve her mother in law, Naomi. It was risky and it took courage. And Naomi's heart was to help Ruth find love and security.

Only the creativity of God would tell Ruth to wait until the eligible bachelor Boaz was a little intoxicated. She was then to go to him late at night and show him that she was "available for marriage" in a most respectful way.

Oh my! Release the expectations of how your story *should* play out, and open your heart and spirit to the creative directives from the Holy Spirit.

I am not advocating that women pursue men aggressively, because I still believe it is healthier for both men and women when the men are initiating and pursuing. At times I have taken matters into my own hands, and it backfired terribly. No, I am simply saying that we need to be open to the voice of the Holy Spirit.

Declarations

Thank you, Lord, that Your ways are higher than our ways. We trust You with all of our hearts, and we lean not on our own understanding. Thank you for Your faithfulness. And (as my mother would say) we stand on tiptoe waiting with expectancy to see what You are going to do! We submit to You, Father God, Jesus, and Holy Spirit.

1. We declare that we have ears to hear Your voice above all others; that we will obey Your directions no matter how unconventional. (See Matthew 11:15.)
2. Impart to us kindness, so while we are waiting for that moment with our Boaz (or Ruth), we will serve others with kindness and grace.
3. Lord, we declare the men (or women) You have chosen for us will feed on Your Word; and they will be filled with the new wine of the Holy Spirit.

4. We declare the intoxication of the Spirit to come over the men who are called to marriages—filling them with cheer and joy! Wash away their disappointments and the cares of the world with the new wine. Cause them to lie down in submission to Your Holy Spirit, and rest with You. (See Ruth 3:7.)
5. We command that anything covering or hiding the men and causing them to be complacent be removed in Jesus' Name. And Lord, make the men uncomfortable—give them a chill in the night—that they will notice someone is missing until they *awake* to meet their wives. (See Ruth 3:7.)
6. We declare that when the men awake, the women will have the boldness, courage and trust in You Lord to identify themselves as their wives—according to Your unique instructions. (See Ruth 3:9.)
7. We declare the word Boaz spoke over Ruth: "Fear not!" We are known as virtuous women; women of strength—worthy, brave and capable. (See Ruth 3:11.)

Amen! Expect to be amazed!

Day 18
Honor and Forgive

While working on this prayer project, I noticed a new pattern with the men I was meeting and personal things they were sharing with me. Two men had nearly an identical story. Neither had been married, both were close to the age of 50, and they were angry with their fathers—partly because of how their fathers treated their mothers. Another man was going through a divorce, and he was struggling to forgive several people in his life—especially his former wife—an alcoholic who refused to get treatment.

I wondered: *Why these particular men, and why now?* The answer arrived in my email inbox early the next morning from my sister, Lisa, about honoring and forgiving our parents. This is such an important topic to address when preparing for marriage.

> Nurse resentment and you are never released; forgive your parents for the past or the past forever holds you – (you become) the permanent child.
>
> I don't do this well. And I've got to figure out how—how to honor the parent; because didn't God promise that without that nothing else can go well?
>
> It's only forgiveness that gives a future. Ann Voskamp[1]
>
> Honor your father and mother, as the Lord your God has commanded you, that your days may be long, and that it may be well with you in the land the Lord your God is giving you (Deuteronomy 5:16).

Forgiveness releases the other person (and you) from your need to punish them. "But if ye forgive not men their trespasses, neither will your Father forgive your trespasses..." (Matthew 6:9-13, KJV).

Forgive past relationships. The Lord will vindicate you when you release those who have hurt you. Further, trust that God will take care of the other person while you let go and move forward in your life.

Vindicate me, O Lord; For I have walked in my integrity. I have also trusted in the Lord; I shall not slip. Examine me, O Lord, and prove me; Try my mind and my heart. For Your loving kindness is before my eyes, And I have walked in Your truth (Psalm 26:1-3).

Let us pray and make declarations for ourselves, the Holy Spirit will lead all of us to forgive people in our lives and honor our parents. Prayerfully pause at each "station" below to listen. Let the Holy Spirit speak to you now.

Declarations

Thank you, Lord Jesus, that You took all of our pain, wounds, resentments and un-forgiveness and crucified them on the cross. By Your shed blood, we are cleansed and restored; we are forgiven. Your mercies are new *every* morning.

1. Father God, we declare Your perfect love is surrounding and encompassing us and the men and women called to marriages. Your perfect love drives out all fear. (See 1 John 4:18 NIV.)
2. Lord God, reveal all the ways in which we have not honored our parents: Forgive us Lord for not honoring or respecting our parents. They are Your gift to us. Release Your Spirit and the anointing of forgiveness now.
3. We declare that as we have been forgiven by our heavenly Father, we forgive our parents for their failures, shortcomings, and in all the ways they have wounded our hearts.
4. We declare the eyes of our hearts are enlightened to see the other people we need to forgive. You are the Lord; and the God who forgives us as we forgive those who have sinned against us. (See Luke 11:4.)

DAY 18

5. We bless those who have cursed us; taking every careless or damaging word spoken to us, over us, or about us, captive; and we send back blessings.
6. We declare a release of the Father's blessing to each person for whom we are praying. Heal, restore, and bless each of us with the Father's perfect love.
7. Thank you, faithful Lord, for acting on our behalf as we declare Your mighty words.

For the Lord (of the breakthrough) will rise up as at Mount Perazim.... That He may do His work, His awesome work, And bring to pass His act, His unusual act (Isaiah 28:21).

Day 19
You Are Worthy

Do you ever struggle with knowing you are worthy of the love of a fine man or woman of God? I do. Feeling that I am worthy of the great things God has for my life has been one of my greatest struggles, though it is more subconscious than conscious. Rejection takes a hit on our sense of worthiness and value, like a beautiful gold crown that has been kicked to the curb and forgotten.

Rejection will come—through romantic relationships, friendships, and work or church relationships. As my mother has often said, "All people will let you down at some point; only God will never leave you or forsake you."

One friendship "situation" happened during the process of writing and posting to the blog, *1 + 1 = One*. Though now I don't remember specifics, it's a good example of what we experience at some point in our lives—or several points. My girlfriend was sharply critical of me, and for two nights I allowed tormenting thoughts to hang out in my mind. The relentless voice was not the voice of God; it was the enemy taunting me with critical words spoken through a "friend." I began to analyze *all* my relationships and seeing *all* the things I did wrong. I was feeling unworthy of love, believing the lies, and agreeing with the criticism.

But God!

On nights like those, when the negative thoughts are parading around in my mind, the noise will not stop until I take control of the situation. My greatest counter attack is simply to speak the name of Jesus, out-loud. *Jesus.* Jesus! And sleep returns.

DAY 19

It is a discipline, a choice, to pull yourself out of the swirling waters and back to the stillness of dry ground to gain perspective.

> **We demolish arguments and every pretension that sets itself up against the knowledge of God, and we take captive every thought to make it obedient to Christ (2 Corinthians 10:5 NIV).**

Making declarations is so important *because* the enemy only comes to steal, kill, and destroy, (see John 10:10). The accuser of the brethren (see Revelation 12:10) enjoys whispering lies to our hearts and minds. He attacks our identity and delights in our downward spiral into feelings of unworthiness.

The Word of God is sharper than a two-edged sword; it is a powerful weapon of our warfare. Faith comes by hearing the Word of God spoken by our own voices, to our conscious and subconscious selves. Declaring the truth over the lies will bring the victory.

The truth is that you are a child of the King of kings, and *you are worthy* of love, worthy of success, and worthy of the call of God on your life.

Make these declarations because you need to hear and *believe* in your value and worth. I don't know about you, but though I understand that I am worthy of God's love, there was a time in my life when I struggled with knowing the truth in the depth of my heart. The dings of rejection can bruise our sense of worthiness. Some of the declarations may seem repetitive, but it will be good for your spirit and heart to hear these words of truth!

Declarations

(Men – please adapt these declarations.)

Thank you, Father God, for Your love for me. I choose to agree with Your Word and Your opinion of me, because You have created me for greatness! Marriage is Your design and plan.

1. I declare *I am worthy* to be loved by God's *best* man—a man of valor and a man after God's own heart.

2. I declare I am a woman of strength, worth, bravery and capability. (See Ruth 3:11 AMP.)
3. I declare I am an intelligent, and virtuous wife; and the man You have chosen as my husband will find me.
4. I declare I am more precious than jewels, and my value is far above rubies, pearls or diamonds. (See Proverbs 31:10 AMP.)
5. The heart of my husband will safely trust in me confidently, and he will rely on and believe in me securely, so he has no lack of [honest] gain. (See Proverbs 31:11 AMP.)
6. I declare I am a virtuous and worthy wife [earnest and strong in character] and a crowning joy to my husband! (See Proverbs 12:4 AMP.)
7. I choose to take my negative thoughts captive, and use God's mighty weapons to knock down the strongholds of human reasoning and to destroy false arguments. I am worthy! (See 2 Corinthians 10:4-5 NLT.)

Thank you, Lord, that where I (the crown) have been tarnished and bruised, You are the God who *restores*, and You have restored me to worth and value above that of a royal crown.

Amen! Expect to be amazed!

Day 20
God Has Not Forgotten You

You, my friend, are *worthy of love*. You are worthy of God's best. God is a God of excellence, so He will not skimp, and He has not forgotten you!

> To some it may seem like God has forgotten about His promise for the right marriage for you. In reality, God is lining things up and wants the best for you. Timing is everything. God does not want you to suffer or perish. He does not want to settle for less. Wait on Him and in time He will give you all that He has promised to you. (See 2 Peter 3:8-9.) Doug Addison[1]

> Sing for joy, O Heavens! Rejoice, O earth! Burst into song, O Mountains! For the Lord has comforted his people and will have compassion on them in their suffering. Yet Jerusalem says, "The Lord has deserted us; the Lord has forgotten us." (He says) "Never! Can a mother forget her nursing child? Can she feel no love for the child she has borne? But even if that were possible, I would not forget you! See I have written your name on the palms of my hands" (Isaiah 49:13-16 NLT).

"God is the God of romance!" is a phrase we use in my family because we have witnessed God's romantic hand in bringing the couples in my family together. The testimonies are so intricate and wonderful that my sister is writing a book. My two older sisters were married in their early 20s, my brother a few years later, each with divine, interwoven love stories. And our parents, oh my, they have the most romantic story of all, and they are now the cutest couple—still in love at ages 88 and 91. God is indeed the God of romance.

When my nieces began getting married, I admit I struggled a bit, because in my mind, it was *my* turn for *my* extraordinary love story. With each niece's wedding, and there have been seven to date, plus three of my nephews, I find myself saying, "Hey God! Over here! Have you forgotten about *me?*"

But God does not forget. He has not forgotten about my romance, and He has not forgotten about your love story either. His promises are true; and He does what He says He will do.

God is good, and He is faithful!

Many years ago, when I was living in Aspen, Colorado and not walking the walk, my sister gave me the challenge of my life. Lisa said, "I am going to pray, and then you open the Bible and point and let's see what it says."

Bible roulette!

My reaction was, "Yeah, right. OK, let's do it."

I was certain that I would land on some random page and the words would be meaningless.

To set the stage, we were standing in her condominium in Snowmass, Colorado, overlooking God's majestic mountains with wildflowers everywhere. Gorgeous.

Lisa prayed a short prayer that I paid no attention to and then I opened the Bible. I will never forget it. My finger landed smack dab on Psalm 121:

> **I look up to the mountains – does my help come from there? My help comes from the Lord, who made heaven and earth! He will not let you stumble; The one who watches over you will not slumber....The Lord stands beside you as your protective shade...The Lord keeps you from all harm, and watches over your life (Psalm 121: 1-5,7 NLT).**

Suddenly God was speaking to my heart, and He said, "Barbara. I have had my hand on your life all this time and I have not let your foot slip. I have been protecting you, and even though you have been ignoring Me, I have been walking with you every day. I love you, and I have a great plan for your life."

DAY 20

Wow. God had not forgotten me. And today, He has not forgotten *you* or the men and women for whom you are praying. He has a great plan for each of us. Plans to prosper us in every area of our lives. Plans to give us a future and a hope.

Declarations

Thank you, Father God, that You have not forgotten the desires of our hearts. Thank you for sending the Holy Spirit as our Comforter, and for your compassion for our suffering. Thank you that You are our encourager, and thank you for giving us a fresh dose of hope.

1. We declare that God has not forgotten us, and He cares for the details of our lives. He even knows the number of hairs on our heads. We are of great value to our Heavenly Father. (See Matthew 10:30.)
2. We declare the Lord is watching over our lives, and the lives of those called to marriages. He will not let our feet slip off the right path. He watches over us as we sleep. (See Psalm 121:3 NIV.)
3. We declare what God has spoken, He will act on. What He has promised, He will carry through to completion. (See Numbers 23:19 NLT.)
4. We declare the gifts and call of God regarding marriages are irrevocable. (He never withdraws them once they are given, and He does not change His mind about those to whom He gives His grace or to whom He sends His call.) (See Romans 11:29 AMP.)
5. For He [earnestly] remembered His holy word and promise to Abraham His servant. And God remembers His words and His promises to each of us. (See Psalm 105:42 AMP.)
6. We believe and receive – "I the Lord made you, and I will never forget you! You are written on the palm of My hand!" (See Isaiah 44:21 and 49:16 NLT.)
7. We declare and agree with the prophetic words that God is arranging divine alliances, causing people to come together for marriages.

For He [God]Himself has said, I will not in any way fail you nor give you up nor leave you without support. [I will] not, [I will] not, [I will]

not in any degree leave you helpless nor forsake nor let [you] down nor relax My hold on you! Assuredly not!

So we take comfort and are encouraged and confidently and boldly say, The Lord is my Helper; I will not be seized with alarm [I will not fear or dread or be terrified]. What can man do to me? (Hebrews 13:5-6 AMP)

Amen! Expect to be amazed!

Day 21
What Do I Wear?

There are a lot of girls in my family, with two sisters, a sister-in-law, eight nieces, two niece-in-laws, and my mother. One of the first questions we ask each other when one is going out for a special occasion, and especially a date, is: "What should I wear?" And the next question we ask each other is: "How do I look?"

Esther asked such questions before meeting the king on their first date, and she was given access to the most elaborate closet; far more than you or I could imagine. (See Esther 2:15.) Esther, who had a vision beyond herself, asked for expert advice from the king's custodian of the women, Hegai. He was familiar with the king's tastes, likes, and dislikes, and he knew which garments and accessories would be perfect for Esther, giving her the confidence she needed for her king encounter.

What we wear for any occasion is more than clothing, and when choosing the right outfit, we want clothes that make us feel good inside and out, to look our best and feel beautiful. When we feel we are dressed well, we wear more confidence and the attitudes we wear are more important than pieces of cloth.

Men also spend time choosing the best clothes for a date; appropriate for the occasion; appealing to the lady; comfortable and handsome garments, enhancing their confidence.

Alison Armstrong (one of my favorite relationship authors) in her book, *Making Sense of Men*, says the number one quality that causes men to be attracted to women is self-confidence.

> Self-confidence is the most attractive quality in a woman. It's irresistible. It knocks men over. It draws them in. It makes them feel like what they provide will really make a difference, because she's already fine. She doesn't need rescuing. They can relax. They can be themselves.
>
> Find out what gives you confidence and do it every day. Is it shoes or purses? Manicured nails or a great hair cut? It could be feeling healthy from eating good food. Or feeling fit from taking your body out for a spin. Whatever it is, don't feel guilty about providing it for yourself. Ultimately, your being confident contributes to everyone.
> Allison Armstrong[1]

What gives you confidence?

I feel most confident when I am trusting God, and receiving His perfect love. We are most attractive when we reflect the goodness of the Lord, sparkle with the light of His love, and radiate the fragrance of His presence. God will surround us with His favor, like a shield. (See Psalm 5:12.)

Esther found favor with the king, and because she dressed and adorned herself in garments that would most please him, her confidence radiated, inside and out.

When we wear disappointment, discouragement, self-pity or the evidence of hope deferred, well, it just isn't pretty. We need to do our part to be attractive to the one God is preparing for us.

Let the Lord be the lifter of your head. Take your eyes off your old self, let go of insecurity, and set your gaze on the lover of your soul. Be secure in your identity as a child of the King, and His unwavering love for you.

More of my confidence builders are: A fresh pedicure, working out, eating well, and a visit to the hair salon. But more deeply, I am confident when I spend time focusing on how amazing God is, how He adores me, and who I am because I am a daughter of the King. What are your confidence builders?

DAY 21

Declarations

Thank you, Father, for loving us with Your lavish love! Thank you for being the ultimate lover of our souls. When we receive Your perfect love that drives out all fear, we are free to love the men and women You are bringing into our lives. Speak to us today, and reveal the old rags we cling to that need to be thrown away.

1. We declare that we put off all these old clothes: Bad temper, irritability, meanness, profanity, dirty talk, and gossip. Father God show us any other areas of the old nature that need to be put in the trash. (See Colossians 3:8 MSG.)
2. We declare that now we are dressed in a new wardrobe. Every item of our new way of life is custom-made by the Creator, with His label on it. All the old fashions are now obsolete. (See Colossians 3:10 MSG.)
3. We declare that we are chosen by God for this new life of love. We dress in the wardrobe picked out for each of us: Compassion, kindness, humility, quiet strength, discipline. We are even-tempered, content, and quick to forgive an offense. (See Colossians 3:12-14 MSG.)
4. We declare that we wear *love* above everything else. It is our basic, all-purpose garment and we put it on every morning. (See Colossians 3:14 MSG.)
5. We put on strength, and we put on our beautiful garments. (See Isaiah 61:3.)
6. We put on the crown of beauty instead of ashes, the oil of joy instead of mourning, and a garment of praise instead of a spirit of despair. (See Isaiah 61:3 NIV.)
7. And we thank you, Lord, that You are our provider. We declare the Lord provides *all* our needs; (and sometimes we *need* a new outfit or a mani-pedi).

Amen! Expect to be amazed!

Day 22
How Will You Feel?

Yes, I confess, I have been known to watch *The Bachelor*—usually in snippets—catching moments of the bachelor sorting through the women who, in turn, specialize in catfights. Putting those beautiful women together in a house all focused on winning the affection of one man is just a petri dish for the "uglies" of jealousy, insecurity, fear, and self-pity. Even the most beautiful dress, shoes, smile, and hair will not attract the bachelor in the long-run if the uglies are festering on the inside. Have you seen his face each time a girl starts whining about not spending enough time with him; or about an issue with one of the other girls? Men (and women) tend to be repulsed when the insecurities surface.

I do not do this often enough, but I quiet myself to visualize my future with *the* man. If I see it, and feel it, then I can imagine the steps I need to take to get to the destination. It's a bit like planning a road trip (or getting directions on your GPS). You pick the destination, visualize your arrival, but you must start where you are, knowing where you want to end. Then you can see the roads and turns needed to get you to the destination most efficiently.

Taking the exercise a step further, rather than visualizing the superficial things I *think* I want in a man or a marriage, I imagine how I will *feel*. Not just about being in love, but about my life—emotionally, spiritually, and physically.

How do you want to be feeling in your own skin when you are in a budding relationship with the person you will marry?

How will you feel when you first meet that person?

Here is my list of answers to these questions:

- Accepted and loved by God

- Loving Jesus

- Confident

- Happy

- Passionate about work or ministry

- Healthy

- Secure

- Excited about the future

- Content

- Peaceful

There is no room for the uglies when you feel that good. Perfect love drives out all fear! Receive, and be filled with the perfect love of God, and the fear-based uglies will be driven out of your life. *(See 1 John 4:18.)*

Write a vision of how you feel in your future relationship. Take the time to imagine and *feel* those feelings, and then write the testimony for all of us when it becomes a reality.

Declarations

1. I am accepted and loved by God, and I comprehend more each day the width and length and depth and height of the love of God that surpasses knowledge. (See Ephesians 3:18.)
2. I love the Lord my God with all of my heart, all of my soul, all of my mind, and all of my strength. (See Mark 12:30.)
3. I am confident and happy, because I know the perfect love of the Father, and I have love in my life from others.

4. I am clothed with dignity and strength, and I laugh without fear of the future. (See Proverbs 31:15.)
5. I am not anxious about anything, but in everything by prayer and supplication, with thanksgiving, I let my requests be made known to God. And the *peace* of God, which surpasses all understanding, will guard my heart and mind through Christ Jesus. (See Philippians 4:6-7.)
6. Because of my identity in Christ, I feel confident in my relationships, loved by my heavenly Father, filled with excitement and expectancy for the future, and warmly content *now*.
7. I am confident because God is with me and He surrounds me with a shield of His favor, so I have favor with God, men, and women. (See Psalm 5:12.)

Amen! Expect to be amazed!

Take time to meditate and envision yourself with the person God has for you. How do you look? How do you feel? Write your vision and turn it into a declaration for the next few days, weeks, and months.

Day 23
The Season of Favor

The season of spring is one of new life and beginnings. It is a season of favor and every year I am keenly aware of the bursting forth of *life* in nature as winter gives way to spring. In perfect orchestration, blossoms and flowers explode on cue, inviting us to come out of the confines of a long winter, shed our dowdy grays, and join the celebration.

> **Look around you: Winter is over; the winter rains are over, gone! Spring flowers are in blossom all over. The whole world's a choir— and singing! Spring warblers are filling the forest with sweet arpeggios. Lilacs are exuberantly purple and perfumed, and cherry trees fragrant with blossoms (Song of Solomon 2:11-12 MSG).**

The earth gives us a visual of God's favor in our lives, and before the new life emerges, the dead needs to be shed.

What do you need to shed from the past winters of your life? What are your winter patterns?

It is a process, but I try to be alert and take my old thought patterns captive. Occasionally I am reminded of how things have turned out in the past, and there is a temptation to return to the familiar, cozy, winter blahs. They are the voices of winter telling me to believe that things will turn out as they always have—so just give in or give up.

The truth of today and our futures will only be found by *breaking out* of the patterns of the past, and choosing to leave the false comforts of winter behind. It is a *new* season. Rejoice and believe and see a different outcome for your future!

One of my favorite verses about favor is *"For You, O Lord, will bless the righteous; with favor You will surround him as with a shield"* (Psalm 5:12).

I often pray that God will surround me with a shield of favor. Just recently I focused on this verse:

> **But let all those *rejoice* who put their trust in You; Let them ever *shout for joy*, because You defend (cover) them; Let those also who love Your name *Be joyful in You* (Psalm 5:11).**

I have a choice every day and in every situation. If I

- Rejoice

- Trust God

- Am joyful…

…then I am surrounded by a shield of God's favor, and I am a magnet for good things, and a good man.

Take a few minutes and ask God to show you what the winter patterns are in your mind.

Now shed them.

Open your hearts and minds and give Jesus your doubts, discouragements, rejections, and unbelief.

> **Passionately pursue favor! Why? Because favor is so extremely powerful. Favor will make your life delightful and extremely fruitful for the glory of God. The single blessing of God's underserved, unmerited favor on your life will ensure success in all you do. Patricia King[1]**

Declarations

1. We declare we are breaking out of the winter patterns of our lives, and winter is over and gone. (See Song of Solomon 2:11.)

2. We put on our new springtime garments of celebration! I trade my clothes of mourning in for dancing clothes. You changed my sorrow into dancing. You took away my clothes of sadness, and clothed me in happiness. (See Psalm 30:11 NCV.)
3. We rejoice because we put our trust in the Lord; We shout for joy because God defends and covers us. (See Psalm 5:11.)
4. We declare God blesses the righteous, and He is surrounding us with His Favor as a shield. We declare that our future spouses and others called to Kingdom marriages are surrounded with a shield of God's Favor, and they are attracting us to them. (See Psalm 5:12.)
5. For the Lord God is my sun and shield; the Lord bestows [present] grace and favor and [future] glory (honor, splendor, and heavenly bliss)! No good thing will He withhold from those who walk uprightly. (See Psalm 84:11 AMP.) God is not withholding the good thing of His best spouse from my life.
6. Thank you Lord that Your favor lasts a lifetime. Though my weeping may endure for a night (or winter season), joy comes in the morning. (See Psalm 30:5.)
7. We declare that we will not let loyalty and kindness, mercy and truth, leave us. We tie them around our neck as a reminder, and write them deep within our hearts. Then we will find *favor* with both God and men and women, and we will have a good reputation. (See Proverbs 3:3-4 NLT.)

Amen! Expect to be amazed!

Day 24
Take Courage!

Promise me you'll always remember: You're braver than you believe, and stronger than you seem, and smarter than you think. – Christopher Robin to Pooh

The moment you can visualize being free from the things that hold you back, you have indeed begun to set yourself free. – Unknown

A ski instructor's life is glamorous and exciting. I know, because I lived the life in Aspen, Colorado for five years. Working every day at 8,000' – 12,000' elevation in a state that boasts more than 300 days of sunshine takes its toll on skin. The statistics are one in four ski instructors have skin cancer, and I was one of the four at the early age of 32. I sat in the prep area during the second surgery to remove the cancerous cells around my upper lip and my eye, waiting for another round of needles in my face. I knew I had a choice to make. I could choose to agree with fear, or I could choose to trust God to get me through the surgery. Fear causes more tension, and I knew if I was tense, the needles would be that much more painful, so I chose faith. If Jesus could endure the torture of his scourging and crucifixion for me, I could endure a few needles. It was during that surgery, and because I chose faith over fear, that I experienced waves of the love of Jesus in the most incredible way.

Choosing to believe and trust takes courage.

The key to receiving the promises? Courage!

I can hear the Cowardly Lion now! *"Courage!"*

Do not fear! Do not be discouraged! Do not be dismayed.

DAY 24

"Do not fear" or "fear not" is in the Bible 365 times.

It takes courage to visualize *freedom*!

We need courage to allow God to heal the wounds of the past.

It takes courage to see a vision for the future and to believe again.

It takes courage to hope.

We need courage to let go, and break free from the discouragement.

It takes courage to begin a new relationship.

It takes courage for men to lead.

Choose courage. Take courage and *see* yourself breaking free from the things that are trying to hold you back from the fullness of God's promises and the land flowing with milk and honey.

Declarations

Thank you, Lord, for Your goodness and Your promises of abundance and pleasure. Thank you for imparting to us the spirit of Joshua and Caleb to see the promises in the land flowing with milk and honey. And for the courage and boldness to cross over into the land of our destinies. Thank you, Lord, for Your promise, that You will not leave us or forsake us!

1. We declare the men and women of God called to Kingdom marriages will *arise* and cross over to the promises. (See Joshua 1:2.)
2. We open our spirits, our minds, and our hearts to receive Your command to "Be strong and of good courage." We choose to be bold and courageous. (See Joshua 1:6.)
3. We declare that Your book of the law shall not depart from our mouths. We will meditate on it day and night. We will observe and do according to all that is written in it for then it will make our way prosperous, and then we will have good success. (See Joshua 1:8.)
4. We declare over the other men and women (and to our spirits), "Be strong! Be of good courage! Do not be afraid, nor be dismayed (crack

under stress) for the Lord your God is with you wherever you go!" (See Joshua 1:9.)

5. *Note: Women: Declare these words for the men, and men, declare them for yourselves:*

    Be strong, <u>chazaq</u>; *Strong's* #2388: Be strong, courageous, valiant, manly, strengthened, established, firm, fortified, obstinate, and mighty. Generally the words "strong" or "strengthened" define *chazaq*, but there is a wide range of meaning for this word, which occurs nearly 300 times in the Old Testament. For example, "to encourage," as when David encouraged himself—literally "made himself strong" in the Lord (See 1 Samuel 30:6).[1]

6. We declare that we have eyes to see and visualize our freedom, because where the Spirit of the Lord is, there is freedom. We are free indeed! (See 2 Corinthians 3:17.)

7. We laugh at fear, afraid of nothing! (See Job 39:22 NIV.)

Amen! Expect to be amazed!

Day 25
Now Faith

Now faith is the substance of things hoped for, the evidence of things not seen (Hebrews 11:1).

Faith is the confidence that what we hope for will actually happen; it gives us assurance about things we cannot see (Hebrews 11:1 NLT).

The week I moved my parents from their large home of many years into a 1,050 square foot apartment, my work life was also changing, and one more relationship came to its end.

The door to that relationship had been painfully closed months prior, but I allowed it to crack open again. I was entertaining the possibility of a dramatic change in the ugly situation, because, I told myself, nothing is impossible with God. After a sincere, gushing apology from the guy, I was open to the possibility of trying again with him. He only wanted my friendship, but "just friends" was not going to happen. So I prayed more aggressively the door of that relationship would clearly open or close, and *soon*!

And it did! Quickly the door closed—much to the relief of my family and friends. And I must say I felt tremendous relief, too.

My hope returned with the excitement that God had a much better plan!

If you have been waiting to see the fulfillment of the desires of your heart. And your desire is to be married to God's hand-picked man (or woman) for you, then you might say waiting has been a bit of a trial. "At times you too, have suffered."

We need endurance, encouragement, and we need a fresh dose of *"now faith!"*

> But recall the former days in which, after you were illuminated, you endured a great struggle with sufferings....Therefore do not cast away your confidence, which has great reward. For you have need of endurance, so after you have done the will of God, you may receive the promise: For yet a little while, And He (your husband or wife!) who is coming will come and will not tarry. Now the just shall live by faith; But if anyone draws back, My soul has no pleasure in him (Hebrews 10:32, 35, 37-38).

> But we're not quitters who lose out. Oh, no! We'll stay with it and survive, trusting all the way (Hebrews 10:39 MSG).

Declarations

Thank you, Father God, for a *new* day, and for encouraging us to look to You for our endurance and strength through the waiting.

1. We declare that we perceive the shifting season; we believe that You are moving on our behalf to bring Kingdom marriages together. We now take the steps into the unknown, out of the boat, and onto the water to enter Your good and perfect plan for our lives.
2. We declare that we have *"now faith,"* and the confidence that what we hope for will happen. We have assurance about things we cannot see. (See Hebrews 11:1.)
3. We choose to believe the men and women who You have chosen for each of us are coming to us, and they will not be late. Give them peace, faith and assurance in their wait, too.
4. We stand on tiptoe with anticipation and expectancy to see the next steps in Your great and perfect plan for our lives. And during the wait, we choose to look into Your wonderful face, and focus on the blessings we have, rather than on what we perceive as lack in our lives.
5. We declare we're not quitters who lose out. Oh, no! We'll stay with it and survive, trusting all the way. (See Hebrews 10:32, 35-38; and verse 39 MSG.)

6. We declare that we do not cast away our confidence, which has great reward.
7. For we have need of endurance, so after we have done the will of God, we will receive the promises. (See Hebrews 10:36.)
8. We declare that we have God's gift of faith *now*—the faith that is the confidence that what we hope for will happen. It gives us assurance about things we cannot see. (See Hebrews 11:1 NLT.)

God – You rock!

Amen! Expect to be amazed!

Day 26
God is the God of Restoration

Jeannine, an accomplished world-traveling teacher of spiritual insights, asked God to hide her from men and dating until it was time for her to meet her husband. Twelve years following that prayer, in October of 2010, when she was 39, she was teaching at a conference in Wheatridge, Colorado.

With a ministry group from England was a man named Ian, who had never been to the United States. Ian was excited about his travel adventure, but he was not too keen on staying the extra week his friend insisted he stay. When Jeannine found out he was staying longer, she offered her friendly hospitality to show him the city she adores.

After spending a few days together touring Denver, Jeannine began feeling something she had not felt in 12 years—an electric spark when she was near Ian. Exactly a week after they met—with sparks between them as well as prayers—both Ian and Jeannine knew they were to be married. We call that a "suddenly" of God. Wow! But God!

Ian and Jeannine's marriage is a divine alliance. Their lives together are powerful for the Kingdom of God, and they are giddy-in-love. Sooo giddy!

About a year after the wedding, I had a dream, and though I only remember a few seconds, I believe it was a message of hope from God. In the dream I was talking to Jeannine about her marriage to Ian, and I said to her:

"This marriage is God's restoration!"

DAY 26

The dream was short but poignant, so I knew I needed to look into the word "restoration," rather than relying on my understanding of the word. With my cup of inspiration coffee one morning, I looked up the word "restoration" in my Spirit Filled Life Bible, and found several pages about restoration. One note by James Robison is worth repeating:

"According to the dictionary, 'to restore' means to 'bring back to a former or original condition.' When something is restored in the Scriptures, however, it is always *increased, multiplied* or *improved* so its latter state is significantly better than its original state (see Joel 2:21-26). God multiplies when He restores." [1]

> **Fear not! Be glad and rejoice! For the LORD has done great and marvelous things…Do not be afraid…Be glad…Rejoice in the Lord your God; The vats will overflow with new wine and oil. So I will restore to you the years the swarming locust has eaten….You shall eat in plenty and be satisfied And praise the name of the Lord your God Who has dealt wondrously with you; And My people shall never be put to shame (Joel 2:21-27).**

In the Bible, when there is restoration or renewal, marriage is always a sign of the shift.

In his book *God is a Match-Maker*, Derek Prince explains:

> Restoration of a culture will be marked by restoration of marriage as a source of joy and a cause for celebration. In Jeremiah 33:10-11, God promises the end-time restoration of Judah and Israel: There will be heard once more the sounds of joy and gladness, the voices of bride and bridegroom, and the voices of those who bring thank offerings to the house of the Lord… *"for I will restore* the fortunes of the land as they were before," says the Lord.[2]

The declarations you make through this journey are not just for you and the one waiting for you. We are making agreements for the restorative plans of God. Though I did not realize it throughout the celebrations, Ian and

Jeannine's wedding was a sign that God is bringing restoration to our culture through God's appointed divine alliances.

Be encouraged! Be expectant! *Now* is the time to hope! God is on the move and He has a divine alliance for you, too.

Declarations

Thank you, Lord, for infusing us with hope today. Thank you that You are the God of restoration. Thank you, Lord, that despite what we see in the world around us, or in our circumstances, You remind us not to fear, but to expect the promise of Your restoration!

1. We declare that our God is the God of restoration. (See Acts 3:21.)
2. We declare we do not have a spirit of fear, but of power and of love and a sound mind. (See 2 Timothy 1:7.)
3. We declare we are glad, and we rejoice in the hope of the coming restoration in our lives. (See Joel 2:21-27.)
4. For the Lord says, and we declare, that He will restore the years of destruction, discouragement, and hope deferred. (See Joel 2:25.)
5. We thank you, Lord, for the overflowing new wine, which was the first miracle of Jesus at a wedding. We declare that as in His first miracle at a wedding, God is saving His best for us, and the best is yet to come. (See John 2:10.)
6. We declare God multiplies when He restores and we wait with the expectation that we will see "exceedingly abundantly above all that we can ask or think." (See Ephesians 3:20.)
7. We declare this is a day of restoration, and we will hear an increase of the voices of brides and bridegrooms, which include our own voices as brides and bridegrooms. (See Jeremiah 33:10-11.)

Thank you, Lord, for hearing our prayers, and for Your promise of the restoration of Kingdom marriages!

Amen! Expect to be amazed!

Day 27
The Gift of Bliss

It is a delight to give the perfect gift. When you are excited and confident in the gift you are giving, you take time to wrap it with care, creating a beautiful package, adorning it with ribbons of love.

Receiving a gift is the most fun. Admit it. As children we were far more interested in receiving gifts than giving them. In receiving you must be patient, open your hands, and politely wait for the gift to be handed to you.

When I was a child, my parents created an atmosphere of excitement and anticipation on Christmas morning. My father would hand out the gifts one at a time. Sometimes my mother would put a specific time of day on a gift so we had to wait for the right time to open the special packages.

Waiting and patience are learned skills. When you watch young children with gifts, they reach for the packages before the appointed time, grabbing and ripping them open—even when the package is not a gift for them.

Now think of gift giving in the context of a marriage relationship. *You* are a precious gift; one that will be given to another in marriage.

"Man can only find himself through the sincere gift of self," teaches Christopher West on the *Theology of the Body*. The book written by Pope John Paul II has become known as a revolutionary teaching on the body and sexual love. West wrote a condensed version called *Theology of the Body for Beginners*, and here are a few key snippets:

> Satan's no dummy. He knows that God created the union of the sexes as a sharing in divine life, and his goal is to keep us from this. So he

aims his attack at the very heart of that unity that has from the beginning been formed by man and woman created and called to become one flesh.

The lie he tells you is: "If you want life and happiness; if you want to be 'like God;' then you have to reach out and grasp it for yourself because God sure won't give it to you." [1]

Satan sows doubt into our hearts; we doubt the goodness of our Father God; we reject our "receptivity" and grasp at counterfeits; or we compromise to find happiness.

Christopher West goes on to say that we have freedom in love, and we have the freedom to give our bodies as a gift to another:

> Our bodies have "spousal meaning" because they are capable of expressing divine love, precisely that love in which the other person becomes a gift and - through this gift - fulfills the very meaning of his being and existence.

> The unity – that "one body" – is the purpose of sexual union, in the divine plan: to prefigure in some way the glory, ecstasy, and bliss that awaits us in Heaven (see Ephesians 5:31-32).

> No wonder we are all so darned interested in sex. God put an innate desire in every human being to want to understand it. Why? To lead us to Him. But beware of the counterfeits! Because sex is meant to launch us toward Heaven, the devil attacks right here. When our innate "curiosity" about sex is not met with the "great mystery" of the divine plan, we inevitably fall, in one way or another, for the counter-plan. In other words, when our desire to understand the body and sexuality is not met with the truth, we inevitably fall for the lies. Christopher West [2]

Our God is Rich in Mercy

But God, who is rich in mercy, because of His great love with which He loved us… (See Ephesians 2:4).

If you have fallen for the counterfeits, I remind you that God is compassionate, merciful and kind. Just as Jesus took the shame from the woman caught in adultery (see John 8:2-11), and God received David after his affair with Bathsheba, there is always hope and restoration for you, too. Give your gift of self to Jesus, and let Him wash you with His perfect love, restore you, and set you back on the path that will lead you to your spouse.

"Our supreme calling is eternal ecstasy; unrivaled rapture; bounteous, beauteous bliss!" Christopher West[3]

Declarations

Father God, thank you that we can come to You in our weakness, and You will wash us clean with the blood of Jesus. We have been grasping for happiness and the fulfillment of Your promises. We open our hands, hearts, minds and spirits in faith, to receive the gifts You have for us, including the gift of Your divine nature.

1. We declare men and women called to Kingdom marriages are being transformed by the renewing of our minds through the washing of the Word of God. (See Romans 12:2, and Ephesians 5:26.)
2. We invite Christ to sanctify our sexuality through a life of virtue and by the cleansing blood of Jesus.
3. We declare truth is now revealed and counterfeit lies are exposed; and our spiritual eyes which were blind are now opened.
4. We declare the hearts and minds of those called to Kingdom marriage will release our grasp on the counterfeits. Let them go!
5. We declare that we are a precious gift given to the right person at the perfect time. We will give the gift of ourselves to the person God has chosen to be our mate.
6. We declare the fulfillment of our supreme calling—eternal ecstasy; unrivaled rapture; bounteous, beauteous bliss—on Earth as it is in Heaven!
7. We declare we have been given the spirit of wisdom and revelation in the knowledge and mysteries of Christ. (See Ephesians 1:17.)

Amen! Expect to be amazed!

Day 28
Labels: Barbie and Ken

My college years were memorable, with many great parties on our small campus. For one sorority party, I invited a charming young man named Ken to be my date. Even though I did not know him well, I was so excited at the thought that we would be, could be, Barbie and Ken. Of course, before we had our *one* date, I envisioned us walking down the aisle, Barbie and Ken. Sigh...swoon.

Have you ever known an attractive, powerful man, or a gorgeous woman, and said, "They are the kind of person I want to marry"? I have. Many times. It is good to have high standards when it comes to marriage and to believe that all things are possible with God.

The tricky thing is being open for God's best, and while waiting, not idealizing or idolizing specific people as the "ideal." While praying with a friend one morning, she prayed for me that if I had idealized any men by saying, "He is my ideal man for marriage," the power of my words would be broken. We are not to set our sights on "Ken or Barbie." We are to look to Jesus as our ideal and wait for His best.

Admiring qualities in other people is helpful in creating the vision of your marriage and spouse. We just need to be aware that these are the character qualities of a person we are looking for and not the people themselves. Another area of caution is remembering people we were in relationships with and idealizing that past relationship or person. My friend, it didn't work out for a reason. God closed that door and though He may reopen past relationships, it is best to leave that door for someone else.

Arthur Burke of Sapphire Leadership Group taught a series called "Releasing Singles." He noted one of the ways we need to prepare for marriage (and even if you are married, this is important), is to pray about the labels that others have put on us. Labels we have placed on ourselves. And the labels we have placed on other people.

Labels are the spoken words or vows (declarations) that we have made over ourselves, or words spoken over us by other people.

It may take time, but some of the common labels to be removed from those preparing to be married include *unavailable, already taken,* or *invisible.*

Unavailable or Already Taken:

If someone from your past thought you would be the person they would marry, that person may have casually made a "claim" over you. Arthur Burke believes that when those words have been spoken, your spirit receives the words and projects a message that you are already taken and unavailable. He says that even if you have repented or received ministry, the label still needs to be removed and truth must be spoken over the lies.

Who have you "made claim" over in your life? Is there any person who may have spoken a "claim" over you, leaving you unavailable? I pray this is revealed to you now. The men revealed to me as men I may have idealized, are now married friends, and I admire their marriages. So do not discount a married friend in this process.

Invisible

According to Arthur Burke, there are times when a child may desire to be invisible and makes an inner vow. If there is abuse or strife in the home, or if you have been sexually abused, then you may have made a vow or had the desire to be invisible. This can cause your spirit to be invisible to the spirit of the man or woman God has for you.[1]

Declarations

Father God, thank you for bringing to light Your truth that will set us free. I pray each person making these declarations will be surrounded by the

Comforter—Your Holy Spirit who is the Spirit of Truth. Give us eyes to see and ears to hear Your voice regarding any remaining labels that need to be removed. Thank you, Lord, for your grace and power, and the authority You have given each of us who calls you Lord.

A Guide for your personal prayer:

Father God, please forgive me for making claim over any person in my past as my potential husband or wife; even as *the* ideal husband or wife.

1. I declare the label of my claim as "mine" over the following people _____ is removed now in the name of Jesus Christ. I declare they are available only for Your best spouse for them, and I bless their current or future marriages.
2. I declare any labels of "unavailable or taken" placed on my spirit either by me or someone else, are removed now in the name and by the power of Jesus Christ.
3. I declare I am available to meet and receive God's best spouse for me, in the perfect "suddenly" timing of God.
4. I sever and break any inner vows that I may have made at any time in my life that I am invisible. I declare I am *visible* and I have the favor of God as a shield around my life.
5. I know and declare I am free to walk in the fullness of my destiny, and I am visible and seen by God's best person for me.
6. I am worthy of God's best! I am worthy of the fine people who are successful in all areas of their lives. I am worthy!
7. We pray and declare the labels of *unavailable*, *taken*, or *invisible* placed on our future spouses are removed now in the name of Jesus.

Thank you, Lord, that the veil of invisibility, or unavailability, has been lifted. We celebrate the freedom.

Amen! Expect to be amazed!

Day 29
The Right Place at the Right Time

> If marriage is part of God's plan for you, (and in most cases it is God's plan) then you can trust Him to work out every detail, both for you and for the mate He has destined for you. He will bring you together with a person who is so exactly suited to you that, together, you may experience marriage as God originally designed it. This will be on a level higher than the world has ever dreamed of. Derek Prince, God is a Matchmaker[1]

The bride, Lindsey, had previously been crushed with disappointment when a man she believed was God's husband for her married another woman. *But God* had a better plan for Lindsey. Out of the blue, and despite her waning faith, she met the man of her dreams just after Christmas one year, and they were married the following June.

Lindsey, in her twenties, was giving up, and wondered how she could possibly meet a quality man of God. It is a question we ask. Her friends suggested eHarmony (an internet dating site), but Lindsey was convinced that joining eHarmony was not walking in faith. After losing a bet with her friends, who then put her on eHarmony, Lindsey was in the right place at the right time.

To be positioned for divine appointments requires a heart that is pliable, open, filled with the Spirit of God, and led by the Spirit. We need to hear the still, small voice saying, "This is the way; walk in it...." (see Isaiah 30:21). We need a heart that is tender to the voice of God, and expectant that He is orchestrating the details in our lives so we can walk into His plan and the fullness of our destinies.

For here's what I'm going to do: I'm going to take you out of these countries, gather you from all over, and bring you back to your own land. I'll pour pure water over you and scrub you clean. I'll give you a new heart, put a new spirit in you. I'll remove the stone heart from your body and replace it with a heart that's God-willed, not self-willed. I'll put my Spirit in you and make it possible for you to do what I tell you and live by my commands (Ezekiel 36:24-28 MSG).

And you shall dwell in the land…and you shall be My people, and I will be your God. I will also save you from all your uncleanness, and I will call forth the grain and make it abundant and lay no famine on you. And I will multiply the fruit of the tree and the increase of the field, and you may no more suffer the reproach and disgrace of famine among the nations (Ezekiel 36:28-30 AMP).

Declarations

Thank you, Lord, that we can put our trust in You, and Your best plan for our lives. Thank you, Lord, for communicating with us to know the path to take. And thank you for the confidence to trust that with our eyes on You, we will not miss Your best plan for our lives.

1. We declare Your creative hand is gathering the men and women called to Kingdom marriages to establish us in the right place at the right time—divine appointments for marriages.
2. We submit our lives to You and Your promise to sprinkle clean, healing water upon us; that we will be clean—our filth washed away, and we will no longer worship idols, including the idols of marriage or the ideal spouse. (See Ezekiel 36:24-28.)
3. In agreement with Your Word, we declare our stony, stubborn hearts are removed by Your hand, and we receive new, tender, responsive hearts. (See Ezekiel 36:24-28.)
4. Thank you, Lord, that You have put Your Spirit in each person called to Kingdom marriages; that we will follow Your decrees, and be careful to obey Your regulations. (See Ezekiel 36:24-28 NLT.)

5. We declare multiplication and acceleration. From the testimonies of couples uniting suddenly, we declare the acceleration of divine appointments and meetings; and the multiplication of fruit in our lives—the fruit of marriage relationships.
6. We declare that we have ears to hear Your voice saying, "This is the way; walk in it." (See Isaiah 30:21.)
7. We submit our minds and opinions to You regarding how we will meet our future spouse. We are open to receive new ideas, accept invitations, and Lord, give us strength and freedom to get out of our comfort zone.

Amen! Expect to be amazed!

Day 30
Hawk Night Vision

God is a creative God, and we see His communication in various ways, including through nature. I enjoy long walks with my dogs, and often I see the hawks flying, hunting, and nesting. At certain times of the year they soar in pairs—male and female.

Hawks partner for life. They reside in the same territory throughout their lives, defending it with displays of soaring and diving. One of the amazing gifts God has given these birds of prey is their incredible telescopic vision. The eyes of a hawk are eight times more powerful than a human's. Not only do they see color, but they can see the ultra-violet spectrum as well, seeing and perceiving colors you and I have never seen.

For the person longing to partner for life with God's best, it is imperative that, like the hawks, they see and recognize the person God brings. Keep your eyes up, focus on the Lord and what He's doing in your life, rather than turning your attention inward.

When women take their focus off God's plan, focusing on themselves, the result is often insecurity, which is not pretty. Men who become self-focused tend to be enamored with the man in the mirror, which is equally unattractive.

God is a God of romance, and physical attraction is a gift. I believe His best person for us will knock our socks off in every way. However, many of us need to see beyond physical appearance and allow God to give us eyes to see the whole person.

One of my favorite books on the topic of understanding men and dating is Dan Grey's *Venus and Mars on a Date*. This is what Grey has to say:

DAY 30

> Men tend to have a visual picture of their perfect mate, but rarely is that picture ever correct. It is a fantasy picture of their ideal partner. Not until a man begins to experience real bonding with a woman in a way that makes him feel successful will the power of that picture weaken and be replaced by a real person.
>
> As long as a man has not experienced the reality of making a woman happy, he will compare her with a fantasy picture. He may begin to question his feelings: "I like her, but she is not my picture." As a man continues to know a real woman and feel a real bond of desire, affection, and interest, his need for his partner to look like his fantasy picture subsides. The spell is broken when his heart opens and he feels a special connection with his partner. This process takes time, even if he is with the right person.[1]

It is important to note the fantasy picture dissipates when a man feels he can be successful in making the woman happy. Women—we need to be satisfied with God's love for us, receptive to the gifts a man offers, and appreciative of the man God created him to be. Maintain an attitude of gratitude. See the best, do not be a fault-finder.

Peyton, one of the women in our praying group, shared with me some great insights and wisdom regarding the tendency for men to be self-focused

"My friends recently told me they thought I got in the way of his mirror—the most important person to Joel was Joel. I think he has a good heart but when I take an honest look I can see where they would get that....

"I've realized that only when God is on the other side of that mirror do things and people change. As long as Joel, or Fred, or any other guy, is still looking at himself, he's not going to see all the things that God has for him. Who he is. And he won't be able to give a girl what she deserves because he won't even know what that is."

> Nevertheless when one turns to the Lord, the veil is taken away. Now the Lord is the Spirit; and where the Spirit of the Lord is, there is liberty. But we all, with unveiled face, beholding as in a mirror the

> **glory of the Lord, are being transformed into the same image from glory to glory, just as by the Spirit of the Lord (2 Corinthians 3:16-18).**

A hawk soars with its partner, and together they have a strategic vision for their territory. It's an image of Kingdom marriage, which is vital to the health of society, and a symbol of restoration. The purpose of these declarations is not so all of us can get married and ride off into the sunset. No, you have been called for such a time as this. It is your destiny to partner with the man or woman God has for you. The territory God has given you needs the strength of your marriage partnership to usher in the presence and power of the Kingdom of God. It is time.

Declarations

Thank you, Father God, for speaking to us through Your Creation. Thank you, Lord, that we are partakers of the divine nature, and You have empowered our words to create change as we make declarations. (See 2 Peter 1:4.)

1. We declare we do not conform to the pattern of the world, but we are being transformed by the renewing of our minds. To be able to test and approve what God's will is—His good, pleasing, and perfect will. (See Romans 12:1-2 NIV.)
2. We declare the false images of the "perfect" man or woman, counterfeit, fantasy images—are shattered or burned on the altar of sacrifice.
3. We declare our eyes are sanctified, and we see beyond the surface; that we will see and perceive the "ultraviolet" and the "extraordinary" in other people.
4. We declare that we with unveiled faces are beholding in the mirrors not ourselves, but the glory of the Lord. We are being transformed into the same image (of Christ) from glory to glory, just as by the Spirit of the Lord. (See 2 Corinthians 3:16-18.)
5. We declare that in the fullness of time, we will see, perceive, and know the person God has brought into our lives. And our spirit-man will see, know, and recognize the spirit-man of God's best Kingdom marriage partner.

6. We refute any labels we have put on ourselves and others as "single," and we declare that we are available to be seen as "marriage material" by God's best partner for us.
7. We declare the Kingdom of God has come to the lives of the men and woman called to strategic partnerships of marriage.

Amen! Expect to be amazed!

Day 31
Happiness! Transformed Inside Out

My father is a romantic, and one of the most positive, happy people I know. Always childlike, even in his nineties, he lights up a room, putting a smile on every face. After reading an early draft of this book, it was his suggestion to begin and end the book with the phrase "happily ever after...."

In a whirlwind and giddy romance, my parents met, were engaged, married, and pregnant within six months. So began their wild ride of marriage. Some days, many days, no, *every* day—happiness and love was a choice. Staying married was a choice. And because they chose each other, they survived financial hardship, the death of a child, and many other serious challenges that do not make for happy days. They remained committed, and with God's help, a lot of prayer, and a few miracles, their marriage flourished.

Today, my parents are *so* happy they endured through the years, and they are truly in love. After many years of choosing to see the positive, to be grateful to God, praying together every day, choosing to love, choosing each other…now, they really are living "happily ever after!" I have witnessed first hand God's blessings on their choice to remain committed to God and each other. That's covenant.

> **Marriage isn't just a choice—it's choosing the same person a million times. Danny Silk**[1]

Some will say "happily ever after" is not reality—marriage is difficult and we shouldn't promote fairy tale endings leaving people disappointed. But after

DAY 31

listening to Dan and Linda Wilson teach on their book, *Supernatural Marriage*, I side with my dad and have hope in happy endings.

"Childlikeness is the key to the treasure of supernatural marriage."[2] The Wilsons point out that Jesus tells us to be like little children. We are to have childlike faith. Children love the fairy tales that celebrate good triumphing over evil and the prince always rescuing the damsel in distress. The future in God's story is always happy.

All things are possible. Isn't that childlike faith? Childlike faith believes in happily ever after! As John Eldredge said in the *The Sacred Romance*,[3] the reason we enjoy watching a good film of rescue and romance is because the story is written on our hearts. The union of the Bride, the Church, and the Bridegroom, Jesus, is supernaturally happily ever after!

Jeff Olsen, founder of the Live Happy organization and magazine, emphasizes that happiness is a choice, and you will attract the things you desire in your life when you are happy from the inside out. In marriage and relationships, a man or woman won't make you happy, nor will reaching the goal of marriage.

> **Many people live with the assumption that if they become successful, then they'll be happy. But here's the secret: Happiness is the precursor to success in all areas of life and is easily accessible to everyone. We create happiness by doing a few simple things every day. Jeff Olsen**[4]

My observations of a few simple activities which lead to a "happily ever after" marriage:

1. Praying together and for each other every day.
2. Choosing to be hopeful and positive, knowing that everything will work out.
3. Trusting in God and His goodness and faithfulness.
4. Dancing together—changing sorrow into dancing!
5. Giving and sacrificing for the other person, working together because the two are one.
6. Building a friendship.

I have learned happiness isn't getting what I want, but it is appreciating what I have now, and expressing my gratitude. Gratitude creates happiness and opens us to receive more of the desires of our hearts.

> **She (Wisdom) is a tree of life to those who take hold of her, And happy are all who retain (hold her fast) her. (See Proverbs 3:18.)**
>
> **The wise counsel God gives when I'm awake is confirmed by my sleeping heart. Day and night I'll stick with God; I've got a good thing going and I'm not letting go. I'm happy from the inside out, and from the outside in, I'm firmly formed. You canceled my ticket to hell—that's not my destination! (Psalm 68:8-10 MSG)**
>
> **You changed my sorrow into dancing. You took away my clothes of sadness, and clothed me in happiness. (Psalm 30:11 NC)**
>
> **Happy are the people whose God is the Lord. (Psalm 144:15)**
>
> **By all means, marry. If you get a good wife, you'll become happy; if you get a bad one, you'll become a philosopher. – Socrates[4]**

Declarations

Today, we choose happiness.

Thank you, Father God, for all of Your good gifts. Thank you that You are so faithful, and for Your absolute and lavish love. We are expecting to be amazed with Your gift of "happily ever after" in our lives.

1. We declare the people You are bringing together for powerful partnerships love You with all of their mind, heart, soul, and strength. They believe and know You are good and faithful.
2. We declare we are happy from the inside out, and from the outside in. We are firmly formed by You, God. (See Psalm 68:10 MSG.)
3. Thank you, Lord God, that You changed our sorrow into dancing. You take away our clothes of sadness and clothe us in happiness. (See Psalm 30:11 NC.)

4. We declare we are happy because God is our Lord. (See Psalm 144:15.)
5. We take hold of Wisdom, a Tree of Life, and happy are those of us who retain (hold fast) to her. (See Proverbs 3:18.)
6. We choose to live a happy life, keeping our eyes open for God – we watch for Your works, and we are alert for signs of Your presence! (See Psalm 105:3-4 MSG.)
7. Lord God, You are the happiest of happy. Thank you for leading us, and for connecting us to our "happily ever after."

Amen! Expect to be amazed!

Day 32
Expect the Best

Waiting patiently is not an easy thing

My mind buzzing with what could be

With a heart that aches, anticipates

Like a groom, in your waiting room

From your balcony you'll be glittering

Your eyes dancing all over me

Come sweet liberty, come and turn the key

To this room, waiting room.

Waiting Room – Justin Dillon, Tremelo[1]

I love the image of "from your balcony, you'll be glittering, your eyes dancing all over me" and I am really looking forward to that day in my future. Can you feel her excitement and anticipation—the expectancy? There is no doubt.

The challenge in waiting is remaining full of hope, and daily expecting God's best. When we don't see answers to our prayers and heart's desires, we begin to change our expectations. I fight the tendency to expect rejection—the thought that if I am prepared for it, then it will not be as painful. Yes, it has been my experience, so I must strain to return to that balcony as an expectant, hopeful bride-to-be, with no doubt in sight.

DAY 32

If you have been waiting for the right man or woman for any length of time, you have probably heard people say, "your expectations are too high!" or "you are *too* picky!"

What is the right way to wait and hope and expect? Our expectation needs to be focused on God. We also need to have a vision of the thing hoped for, and trust that God will give us *"exceedingly, abundantly above all that we could ask or think"* (see Ephesians 3:20).

"Write the vision...though he tarry, wait for him" (Habakkuk 2:3). God delights in our steadfast faith that believes that He is a good Father, and that He wants to give us the desires of our hearts. We have a choice—to believe and see the best, or to doubt the goodness of God.

> **But let him ask in faith, with no doubting, for he who doubts is like a wave of the sea driven and tossed by the wind (James 1:6).**

Another little book that has helped to shift my hope and expectations—one of the treasures from my mother's library—is *The Power of Positive Thinking* by Norman Vincent Peale:

> **William James, the famous psychologist said, "Our belief at the beginning of a doubtful undertaking is the one thing (now get that – the one thing) that ensures the successful outcome of your venture." When you expect the best, you release a magnetic force in your mind, which by a law of attraction tends to bring the best to you.**
>
> **This does not mean that by believing you are necessarily going to get everything you want or think you want. Perhaps that would not be good for you. When you put your trust in God, He guides your mind so you do not want things that are not good for you. But it does mean that when you learn to believe, that which has seemingly been impossible moves into the area of the possible. Every great thing becomes for you a possibility.**
>
> **It is a well-defined and authentic principle that what the mind profoundly expects, it tends to receive.**[2]

"Therefore I say to you, whatever things you ask when you pray, believe that you receive them, and you will have them." (See Mark 11:24.)

I know, reading the above might tweak your religious side a bit. I pray you hear what the Holy Spirit is saying to you. After much disappointment and waiting, do you expect the best? Do you need to take your thoughts captive? What do you expect in your heart of hearts? It is time to transform your expectations to hope!

Declarations

Thank you, Lord God, that You are the God of hope! Search our thoughts and our hearts, and uncover any patterns of negative self-talk. Reveal to us inner doubts we may have in Your goodness and plans for our lives. Wash us with Your Word, and transform us by the renewing of our minds.

1. We declare that today we expect the best, and with God's help, we will attain the best.
2. We declare our souls wait only upon God and silently submit to Him; for our hope and expectations are from Him. He only is our Rock and our Salvation; He is our Defense and our Fortress. We shall not be moved. (See Psalm 62:5-6 AMP.)
3. We declare we wait for the Lord; our souls wait; and in His Word, we hope and have our expectation. (See Psalm 130:5.)
4. We declare in You, Lord, we put our trust; Let us never be put to shame. The Lord God is our hope and our expectation. (See Psalm 71:1,5.)
5. Since we have such a glorious hope; such a joyful and confident expectation; we speak and declare freely, openly and fearlessly. (See 2 Corinthians 3:12 AMP.)
6. We declare we hope for what we do not see, and we eagerly wait for it with perseverance. (See Romans 8:25.)
7. We declare hope and expectancy is restored; and God is breaking through in the area of Kingdom marriages. He is the Breaker!

Amen! Expect to be amazed!

Day 33
False Summits

Have you ever hiked a big mountain, or ridden your bike an excruciatingly long distance? Or perhaps you love to run and have competed in a marathon or half marathon; or a triathlon—an experience not on my bucket list. Then you must know the feeling of a journey that began with enthusiasm, and evolved into a grueling, painful, and long trudge. At some point you see the end in sight, and exclaim at last…"I can do this! Just a few more steps, around the bend, and just over that next hill…," but the sinking disappointment hits when you realize it was a false summit. You realize you must find the strength, courage, and hope for enduring the pain of the journey again. "Just a little bit further" has become much longer than you anticipated.

Unprepared and ill-equipped, I set out on a hike with some friends one June day. I was planning to turn around midway, but, encouraged by the glance of the man I was with, I chose to continue and we hiked and summited the highest peak in Colorado, Mt. Elbert, at 14,482 feet elevation. Before celebrating our accomplishment at the summit, my group of four paused to estimate the time remaining based on what we could see of the trail and that massive mountain. We pushed our tired bodies to the point appearing to be the top, but we were met with disappointment when we realized we were looking at a false summit—a counterfeit.

Do you see where I'm going? I'm talking about meeting counterfeits to the person you believe God is bringing into your life—the long-awaited desire of your heart—your dream. Ironically, I was on that hike with one of those counterfeits, so it is a feeling I am familiar with, and I hear the same kinds of stories from friends.

God, I don't know if I can go any further! I don't know if I can meet one more counterfeit to the man I hope to marry.

But God has created us with an amazing ability to rebound, to find the strength and courage to hike to the real summit, even if it takes much longer than is comfortable. He didn't say our life's journey would be comfortable. He said He is faithful, He is good, and He will never leave us or forsake us.

Some of the verses I was speaking (declaring!) on our big mountain adventure are just what you might need to continue your journey to your dream of a Kingdom marriage. Oh, but first the lyrics to "Climb Every Mountain," which I was singing as I hiked, not realizing how perfect the words were for this present quest. We are waiting for the dream that will require all the love we can give for as long as we live:

> **Climb every mountain, Search high and low, Follow every byway, every path you know. Climb every mountain, Ford every stream, Follow every rainbow, Till you find your dream. A dream that will need, All the love you can give, Every day of your life, For as long as you live.**[1]
>
> **Righteousness will go before Him, And shall make His footsteps our pathway (Psalm 85:13).**
>
> **The Lord God is my Strength, my personal bravery, and my invincible army; He makes my feet like hinds' feet and will make me to walk [not to stand still in terror, but to walk] and make [spiritual] progress upon my high places [of trouble, suffering, or responsibility]! (Habakkuk 3:19 AMP).**

I encourage you to hope today, and tomorrow, because God is good, and He *is* faithful.

Take the next step. God's promises will be fulfilled!

Declarations

Thank you, Father God, that You are good and You are faithful. You even showed Moses Your great goodness when he asked You to show him your

DAY 33

glory. Show us Your glory, Lord God. Show us Your goodness. We are grateful for Your incredible love and presence in our lives.

1. We declare we have a vision that is yet for an appointed time, and the vision will not deceive or disappoint. Though it tarry, we are waiting earnestly for it, because it will surely come on its appointed day. (See Habakkuk 2:3 AMP and NKJV.)
2. We declare we are equipped with endurance, so after we have done the will of God, we will receive all that He has promised. (See Hebrews 10:36.)
3. We declare the Lord's righteousness goes before Him, making His footsteps our pathway. (See Psalm 85:13.)
4. We declare the Lord God is our strength, our personal bravery, and our invincible army. He makes our feet like hinds' feet and will make us to walk [not stand still in terror, but to walk] and make [spiritual progress upon the high places of trouble, suffering, or responsibility]! (See Habakkuk 3:19 AMP.)
5. We declare we will climb every mountain, search and follow, until we find our dream. A dream that will need all the love we can give, all the days of our lives, for as long as we both shall live.
6. We declare we are strong, vigorous, and courageous. We are not afraid, nor dismayed, for the Lord our God is with us wherever we go. (See Joshua 1:9 AMP.)
7. I focus on this one thing, forgetting the past and looking forward to what lies ahead. I press on to reach the end of the race to receive the heavenly prize for which God, through Christ Jesus, is calling me. (See Philippians 3:13-14 NLT.)

Amen! Expect to be amazed!

Day 34
Believe and Receive

It is more blessed to give than to receive (Acts 20:35).

A true statement, and the context is speaking of money, but we can get out of balance. Especially for women, it is much *easier* for us to be busy giving, doing and striving, than it is for us to sit back, wait, and receive. In my spiritual journey I need to stop telling God what He *should* be doing. I need to step back from my busy life to *receive* the love and wisdom He is trying to lavish on me.

Receive His Love.

He breathed on them, and said to them, "Receive the Holy Spirit" (1 John 3:22). Receive from the Lord, Your King, Father, and the Lover of your soul. We need to be refreshed and filled up again and again. When I want to receive from God, I posture myself with open arms, open hands, and open heart and spirit. He is a safe place and I trust Him.

We pray, "God give me: peace, power, provision, wisdom, faith, love, healing, a sign, a word, favor, and a spouse." Often I will pray for something I need. Then without pausing to receive what He has made available to me, I rush into the day hoping God will do something.

After the patterns of heartache and disappointment, I find it challenging to open myself up to receiving mode, both in my relationship with God, and other people—particularly the men in my life. Receiving is an important part of relationship with another person, but it may feel vulnerable, risky, and a bit out of our control.

DAY 34

In the book *Making Sense of Men*, Alison Armstrong shares her insights about men, and "the goods that attract a man." Yes, physical appearance is the beginning, but she says men are most attracted to a woman's confidence, passion, authenticity, and *receptivity*. I don't know about you, but it is much easier for me to shift into *give* mode when I am interested in a man. I've had to *learn* to receive and appreciate what the men in my life offer me—including my father.

Armstrong notes:

> There are two kinds of receptivity that men need, and they can't live without either of them.
>
> The first kind of receptivity men need is women being open and responsive to all the ways they express caring for us…in how they take care of us, protect us, contribute to us and make us happy. These are gifts they offer, and they need women to be receptive to them.
>
> The second kind of receptivity men need is even harder for contemporary women to provide. Men need women to be receptive to who they are. The way one man said it was, "There's nothing like looking in a woman's eyes and seeing that she accepts you." [1]

A woman's receptivity of a man, for who he is and what he offers to her, is not only attractive to him, but it is an essential piece of a healthy relationship.

"The woman will encompass the man." (See Day 16 and Jeremiah 31:22.)

Encompassing is embracing; it is receiving *who* a man is, seeing the best, and accepting him.

You are praying for marriages and your future spouse. A question to ponder is, are you open to receiving the answer to your prayer from God and to make room for that person in your life?

Jesus is telling His disciples there is power in the words we speak.

"Say…believe…receive!"

And whatever we ask *we receive* from Him, because we keep His commandments and do those things that are pleasing in His sight (1 John 3:22).

So Jesus answered and said to them, "Assuredly, I say to you, if you have faith and do not doubt, you will not only do what was done to the fig tree, but also if you say to this mountain, 'Be removed and be cast into the sea,' it will be done. And whatever things you ask in prayer, believing, you will receive" (Matthew 21:21-22).

Receive, I pray you, the law and instruction from His mouth and lay up His words in your heart (Job 22:21-22 AMP).

Declarations

Father God, we choose to receive from You, and we pray for the men and women preparing for partnerships to *receive* from the opposite genders in their lives. We open ourselves to You today to receive Your revelation. We ask You to reveal and remove the old mindsets. And we remove our protective outer garments—we remove the veils we hide behind.

Breathe on us now.

1. We declare that we *receive* the Holy Spirit. Fill us Lord. Refresh us. Touch every dry place in our beings. (See 1 John 3:22.)
2. We declare that we *receive* Your perfect love that drives out *all* fear. (See 1 John 4:18.) We let go of fear, and trust You to be our protector; our shield.
3. We declare that we *receive* Your power...and we *say* to the mountains of (your list of obstacles here), "Be removed!"
4. As we receive from You, Lord, and acquaint ourselves with You, we are at peace knowing that we will prosper, and great good is coming to us. (See Job 22:21.)
5. We declare that we *receive* the instructions from Your mouth and Your Word and we lay them up in our hearts. (See Job 22:22.)

6. We declare that we will trust You Lord, and receive the person You are bringing into our lives. We accept who they are, and see all that You have called them to become now and in the future. We receive Your best.
7. We choose to receive one another, just as Christ also received us to the glory of God. (See Romans 15:7.)

Thank you, Lord. We love You.

Amen! Expect to be amazed!

Day 35
Praying for Your Friends

> **And the Lord restored [turned the captivity of Job – what was captured from Job] Job's losses when he prayed for his friends. Indeed the Lord gave Job twice as much as he had before (Job 42:10).**

Sometimes in the drudgery of our own waiting, we lose perspective and understanding of the many other people waiting and praying for God's divine intervention in their lives. One Sunday at church, a lovely lady with white hair and crystal blue eyes prayed for me, and she told me that she too was waiting and praying for breakthrough in her life. Tears began to pool around her eyes, and I could see she knew "hope deferred." As she prayed and gave her faith on behalf of my concerns, I saw God bringing abundant restoration to her. I heard myself say, "as you give to others through your prayers, it will be given to you."

> **Give, and it will be given to you. A good measure, pressed down, shaken together and running over; will be poured into your lap. For with the measure you use, it will be measured to you (Luke 6:38 NIV).**

As I have battled worry, doubt, and unbelief, which all direct my focus onto myself, I remind myself of Job, and choose to "pray for my friends." Job's friends were dishonest and disheartening, so if you have friends like Job's, pray for them. Tugging on my heart is not only to pray for others who are struggling, or to bless those who curse us, but to pray for the people in our lives who are blessed. I sometimes need a reminder to pray for friends who have a great marriage, wonderful children, and a steady income. I praise God for those who are walking in the fullness of their hopes and dreams—the epitome of the desires of my own heart.

Is there sometimes a sharp pang in your heart when you see your friends blessed with the things that you have been praying for? Oh, the slippery slope of self-pity, and we've all been there.

The remedy? Pray for your friends. Pray for more blessing on those who seem to have it all.

> **Rejoice with those who rejoice (Romans 12:15).**
>
> **Give and it will be given to you (Luke 6:38).**

Praying for your friends is not a formula to get double restoration from God. It is the Kingdom principle of a generous God. When we take our eyes off our own circumstances, and focus on loving our Lord and other people, God restores our faith, hope, and joy.

Who are you going to pray for today? Give the gift of blessing to another. In Chapter 15, we talked about marriage as a mission. Someone else's good marriage is good for all of us, so bless away!

Declarations

> **My response is to get down on my knees before the Father, this magnificent Father who parcels out all heaven and earth. I ask him to strengthen you [my friends] by his Spirit—not a brute strength but a glorious inner strength—that Christ will live in you as you open the door and invite him in. And I ask him that with both feet planted firmly on love, you'll be able to take in with all followers of Jesus the extravagant dimensions of Christ's love. Reach out and experience the breadth! Test its length! Plumb the depths! Rise to the heights! Live full lives, full in the fullness of God (Ephesians 3:14-19 MSG).**

Father God, I pray for my friends and for the marriages around my life; for _____, that You will bless their socks off.

1. We declare the Lord is strengthening marriages, increasing love for one another, and more love for God. Give them Your love, Lord, and joy overflowing, so rivers of living water will pour out on their communities and all who come in contact with them.
2. We declare the couples are surrounded and filled with the gift of romance, and the Lord is giving them divine wisdom to keep Jesus at the center of their relationships.
3. We declare their families are protected, and their children are empowered to walk even closer with Jesus as their Lord and Savior.
4. We declare increase to their financial blessings that they will be able to give more then they ever dreamed possible.
5. We declare the Holy Spirit is visiting them with dreams and visions for the Kingdom, which are your plans for their lives together. Give them a spirit of wisdom and revelation in the knowledge of God. (See Ephesians 1:17.)
6. We declare and agree with God's Word, that as we give, it will be given to us. A good measure, pressed down, shaken together, and running over will be poured into our lap. For with the measure we use, it will be measured to us. (See Luke 6:38 NIV.)
7. Now to Him who, by the power that is at work within us, can do superabundantly, far over and above *all* that we ask or think. To Him be glory in the church and in Christ Jesus throughout all generations forever and ever. Amen! (See Ephesians 3:20 AMP.)

God can do anything, you know, far more than you could ever imagine or guess or request in your wildest dreams! He does it not by pushing us around but by working within us, his Spirit deeply and gently within us (Ephesians 3:20-21 MSG).

Amen! Expect to be amazed!

Day 36
What's He (She) Got?

Out of the blue one day, I received a text message from a man who had captured my interest a year before. We had been on a few dates, and I thought we were progressing nicely, although slowly, until he called to cancel a date and to say, "I just don't feel a deep connection." (See the introduction to this book.)

I thought we needed to spend more time together to develop a deeper connection, so I suggested we remain friends, and we did—until he found Cindy on an Internet dating site. Have you ever maintained a friendship with a man or woman you secretly hoped would wake up one day and know that you're the one? I have. And I don't recommend allowing someone who is not interested in a romantic relationship with you to occupy your time, when God has so much more for you. Still, we need to be sensitive and caring about our friendships with the opposite gender because sometimes they are interested in a future romance with you. It is a delicate dance.

A few months after we decided to be "just friends," I was invited to go skiing with that man, his best female friend, *and* his latest Match. com date! My true heart for him was revealed to me when I found myself uncomfortable with other women swooning around him. I was surprised his date, Cindy, had a similar stature to me, and I quickly shifted to find-Cindy's-flaws-mode. I decided that their relationship would not last long.

I was *so* wrong about Cindy. Their relationship became serious, and lasted many months. When I met her, I looked for the reasons their budding relationship would not last. Deep down I maintained the hope he would wake up attracted to all of *my* great qualities, even though that was not God's plan.

"What's she got that I ain't got...?"

"She's got you, that's what she's got, that's what she's got!"

We have all asked that question voiced in this 80s song by the Producers. (The YouTube video is entertaining!)

Yes, I replayed the few dates I had with "Tall Dark and Handsome," trying to figure out where I blew it, and what's she got that I ain't got? My wise-self finally screamed, "*stop it,* and be thankful God closed that door!"

> **The enemy of faith is not unbelief, it is memory; because memory is the record of what has already taken place, whereas faith is the revelation of what is yet to happen. Even good memories can be bad if they keep us from believing God for something better by enticing us to settle for the good we know instead of for the best we have not tasted yet. Ed Silvoso[1]**

Do I trust God? Or not? One of my favorite prayers when I meet a new man of dating/marriage potential is Isaiah 22:22: "Lord, thank you for Your purposes for ____ in my life. If this relationship is from You, then open the door that no one can shut. And if this man is not good for me, close the door that no one can open!"

Sometimes the door closes quickly and, after the initial blow, I remember my prayer and thank God for protecting me from what I cannot see.

Save yourself from the time-wasting agony of rehashing the past, comparing yourself to others, or trying to figure it all out. Of course we need to be open to learn valuable lessons from our experiences, but you know what I'm talking about.

> **Comparison is the death of joy. Mark Twain[2]**

Trust God. He is worthy of our faith and trust. He is good, and He will honor His promises. Trust Him enough to release your past disappointments, accept the way things worked out, and look with faith and expectancy

DAY 36

to the great things He has for your future. Do not get entangled in your memories. Give thanks with a grateful heart for all the doors that close, and prepare yourself for the doors God is about to open to His best for you.

Get ready! He's going to knock your socks off!

> Trust (lean on, rely on, and be confident) in the Lord and do good; so shall you dwell in the land and feed surely on His faithfulness, and truly you shall be fed. Delight yourself also in the Lord, and He will give you the desires and secret petitions of your heart. Commit your way to the Lord [roll and repose each care of your load on Him]; trust (lean on, rely on, and be confident) also in Him and He will bring it to pass (Psalm 37:3-5, AMP).

> Trust in the Lord with all your heart; do not depend on your own understanding. Seek his will in all you do, and he will show you which path to take (Proverbs 3:5-6).

By the way – I now have a true friendship with the man and his bride-to-be.

Declarations

Thank you, Father, for Your best in my life. I choose today to take my eyes of comparison and judgment off the lives and circumstances of the people around me, and I set my focus on You and Your plan for *my* life.

1. I declare I trust in the Lord with all my heart. I do not lean on my own understanding. (See Proverbs 3:5 NLT.)
2. I declare I seek His will in all that I do, and He will show me which path to take. (See Proverbs 3:6 NLT.)
3. I declare that I have the keys to the Kingdom, and the doors to the best relationships will open that no one can shut; and doors will close to anyone who is not God's best. (See Isaiah 22:22.)
4. This is what the Lord says to all of us who are declaring for Kingdom marriages—his anointed ones, whose right hand he will empower. Before

him, mighty kings will be paralyzed with fear; their fortress gates will be opened, never to shut again. (See Isaiah 45:1 NLT.)
5. This is what the Lord says: "I will go before you, and level the mountains. I will smash down the gates of bronze, and cut through bars of iron. And I will give you treasures hidden in the darkness—secret riches. I will do this so you may know that I am the Lord, the God of Israel, the one who calls you by name." (See Isaiah 45:2-3 NLT.)
6. With the keys, I unlock all areas of my heart, and declare my heart open to God's best. I declare the Kingdom keys are unlocking the heart of my (future) husband or wife, opening their heart to the love of the Father and their future spouse.
7. Praise the Lord! Thank you Jesus for protecting me, and for closing all doors of the past. I thank you for the plans You have for my future marriage. Open wide you heavenly gates so the King of Glory may come in!

Amen! Expect to be amazed.

Day 37
God Delights in Prosperity

Call to Me, and I will answer you, and show you great and mighty things which you do not know (Jeremiah 33:3).

Of the many fears affecting those who desire a great marriage—and even those within present marriages—fear of lack of provision is a biggie. It may be one of the mountains often blocking a future marriage relationship; and it is a common statement that financial stress is the leading cause of divorce.

Even in our modern world of dual incomes, fear around finances affect unmarried men and women. It's a tactic of the enemy to keep people single longer. Men fear not having enough to provide for their wives, a marriage, and a new family, so they may delay the commitment of marriage to get their finances to a certain level. Some of the ladies I know who desire marriage will make a decision about a man based on his income, which is not believing in the God who provides. Are these fear-based decisions slowing the process of meeting the right person?

Financial struggles or concerns tempt us, even seduce us, to take our eyes off our Jehovah Jireh, (The Lord Who Provides), and come into agreement with fear. The Bible says that God *delights* in prospering His people.

> *And the Lord your God will make you abundantly prosperous in every work of your hand, in the fruit of your body, of your cattle, of your land, for good; for the Lord will again delight in prospering you, as He took delight in your fathers (Deuteronomy 30:6-9 AMP).*

On one occasion I was expressing my personal financial struggles and fears to my friend, Debi. She admonished me not to focus on the lack, but to look at the promises of God, and the "Lord who Provides!"

Debi is one of the ladies in my "Texas Ladies Prayer Group;" a group of women I have been praying with every week for several years. Texas was in a severe drought one particular summer, and each week we prayed and asked God to send rain for the drought. "God send Your provision," we cried out… until the day one of the other ladies, Elizabeth, suggested we *bless* the drought.

Bless the drought!

We shifted our prayer focus with an attitude of gratitude and praise; then we blessed the drought and the land of Texas. The rains came a few days later!

Sometimes when we pray about a problem, a relationship, or financial struggles, we are speaking the lack and negative situation over and over again. We magnify the problem rather than focusing on the goodness of God, His promises, and His divine nature to help us when we ask Him. Praying and declaring God's Word and promises will cause us to shift our focus, and set our faces like a flint towards the future and the hope God has promised.

Charles Capps in his booklet *God's Creative Power for Finances* says,

> "The Word of God is not simply a storybook, history book, or religious book. God's Word is creative power. That power is still in the Word, but for it to work for you it must be released by being spoken in faith. Unfortunately, most people are speaking words of fear and failure, speaking often of the depressed economy, lack of jobs, and shortage of finances. They are saying what they have and having what they say."

He goes on to say,

> "I challenge you to change what you are speaking and use your words to bring God's provision into your life. By speaking and confessing these scriptures daily, faith will be created in your heart and you will begin to see God's creative power change the circumstances of your life."[1]

DAY 37

The declarations this week are taken directly from Charles Capps' booklet, *God's Creative Power For Finances*. Speak these Scriptures over your life, and the lives of the men and women (your future husband or wife) called to Kingdom marriages. Make these confessions *daily* until faith comes.

Declarations

God, Your Word says that whatever I bind (forbid) on Earth is bound in Heaven and whatever I loose (allow) on Earth is loosed in Heaven. Therefore, with the authority of Your Word, I bind every force that has set itself against my financial prosperity and the financial prosperity of the men and women called to Kingdom marriages. *I hereby declare all curses against me null, void, and harmless. I am redeemed from the curse of poverty. I am free from oppression.* I now loose the abundance of God and all that rightfully belongs to me to come to me under grace in a perfect way.

1. I am filled with the knowledge of God's will in all wisdom and spiritual understanding. His will is my prosperity (See Colossians 1:19.) God delights in my prosperity. He gives me power to get wealth that He may establish His covenant on the earth. (See Deuteronomy 8:18, and 11:12.)
2. I immediately respond in faith to the guidance of the Holy Spirit within me. I am always in the right place at the right time because my steps are ordered of the Lord. (See Psalm 37:23.) God is the unfailing, unlimited source of my supply. My financial income now increases as the blessings of the Lord overtake me. (See Deuteronomy 28:2.)
3. As I give, it is given unto me, good measure, pressed down, shaken together, and running over. (See Luke 6:38.) I honor the Lord with my substance and the first fruits of my increase. My barns are filled with plenty, and my presses burst forth with new wine. (See Proverbs 3:9-10.)
4. I am like a tree planted by rivers of water. I bring forth fruit in my season; my leaf shall not wither; and whatever I do will prosper. The grace of God even makes my mistakes to prosper. (See Psalm 1:3.) The blessing of the Lord makes me truly rich, and He adds no sorrow with it. (See Proverbs 10:22.)

5. The Lord rebukes the devourer for my sake, and no weapon that is formed against my finances will prosper. All obstacles and hindrances (mountains) to my financial prosperity are now dissolved. (See Malachi 3:10-11 and Isaiah 54:17.) My mind is renewed by the Word of God, therefore, I forbid thoughts of failure and defeat to inhabit my mind. (See Ephesians 4:23.)
6. I am filled with the wisdom of God, and I am led to make wise and prosperous financial decisions. The Spirit of God guides me into all truth regarding my financial affairs. (See John 16:13.) The Lord causes my thoughts to become agreeable to His will, and so my plans are established and succeed. (See Proverbs 16:3 AMP.)
7. There is no lack, for my God supplies all my needs according to His riches in glory by Christ Jesus. (See Philippians 4:19.) The Lord takes pleasure in the prosperity of His servant, and Abraham's blessings are mine. (See Psalm 35:27 and Galatians 3:14.)

Amen! Expect to be amazed.

Day 38
Miss Wiggy Takes a Hike

It was early spring, and time for a BBQ with a small group of friends. Some married, several of us not married—some had never been married, and others had been previously married. As my friend Jenny and I reflected on the evening, I realized there is so much fear driving and paralyzing unmarried Christians who are hoping to have a wonderful Godly marriage.

- Fear of rejection.
- Fear that our "people-picker" will pick the wrong person again.
- Fear of falling off the seemingly narrow path of purity.
- Fear of failure.
- Fear of another chunk of our heart being ripped out.
- Fear of....

You may have heard the phrases *do not fear*, or *do not be afraid* are in the Bible 365 times. *Do not fear* is a message God brings to my attention when I allow fear to be larger than His love. Sometimes God has a still small voice, but other times He makes sure I don't miss His point. You've had this experience too, and in one particular situation it began with awareness and a question: "Do I have *fear* about this potential relationship and man?" Hmmmm... fear? My book-club/Bible-study was talking about fear. Then the presenter at a business meeting was telling us to deal with our fear by doing something that scares us every day. Then my Oswald Chambers book said, *do not fear*; and even the sales book I opened began, "How to deal with your fears."

OK! I hear You God!

My relationship fears sometimes surface like an irritating rash, especially at the beginning of a potential relationship that is teetering on the edge. *I like him; I like him not. He likes me; he likes me not.*

One relationship in particular was challenging in the beginning. The guy was taking me on dates, while he was getting to know another woman. I felt as though I was on an episode of The Bachelor! From my perspective at the time, I believed God had me on a slow path of getting to know the guy to allow my fears to surface, and surface they did! When peace is absent, we need to take our fears or concerns about a relationship to God first. It also helps to be transparent with our friends in prayer, to discern if what we are experiencing are legitimate red flags, or our deep rooted insecurities and fears. Either way, it is important to get back into a place of allowing the peace of God to rule in our hearts. Trust Him, and pay attention.

Back to the relationship that began with a few challenges––did you know that texting a conversation does not always go well and there is a *lot* of room for misunderstanding? As a weekend began, the questionable man was going camping with a church group. I was not invited, and as he was hurrying, we exchanged a few text messages that I interpreted incorrectly. Oh boy. Suddenly my fears were triggered, my insecurities surfaced, and *voila*—I transformed into "Wiggy-Girl," nervously texting things that would have been better left unsaid.

In hindsight, that episode of Wiggy-Girl was amusing, but at the time, it was *so* not funny. I was almost in tears because I misunderstood the text conversation.

Wiggy is a term my friend Jeanie and I use when we fall into the pit of insecurity, and we simply get "wiggy." It is helpful to have a friend who is familiar with those same insecurities––a person who can talk you off the ledge of doing or saying something detrimental to your persona of the faith-filled woman of God.

DAY 38

While the bachelor was camping that weekend, and my texting was under control, I invited God to show me the root of my fears. I realized the anticipated feeling and fear of rejection was all too familiar, and I was leaning into it. Thankful for the revelation, I prayed myself out of the familiar, comfortable zone, knowing the *feeling* was not the truth.

Fear involves torment (see 1 John 4:18). And I was feeling tormented with thoughts of the man choosing someone else. It was the fear of rejection; the dread of starting again. Regardless of the outcome in a situation of uncertainty, God wants us to trust Him. It may be painful in the short term, but trust and know that God is protecting your heart when the other person decides not to choose you.

Coincidentally, at that same time, my Bible study had just finished reading the Beth Moore book, *So Long Insecurity*, and the last chapter sums up the book well:

> **Trust God**
>
> **Plain and simple. Not easy, mind you, but basic and uncomplicated. You don't always have to hash it all out. Sometimes you can make a single swift decision. As Christ said to a wavering disciple, you just have to make up your splintered mind to "stop doubting and believe" (John 20:27). Believe that He loves you and has you covered and takes every one of your hits as if they were aimed at His own skin. Get down to the bottom of what frightens you, and then pitch it to Him like a hot potato.**
>
> **Learn to instantly identify it. Trade it in for trust (in God).**[1]
>
> **She will have no fear of bad news; [her] heart is steadfast, trusting in the Lord. [Her] heart is secure, [she] will have no fear; in the end [she] will look in triumph on [her] foes (Psalm 112:7-8 NIV).**

God bless you with His perfect peace, and may you be set free from your "Wiggy" person today.

Have I not commanded you? Be strong and of good courage; do not be afraid, nor be dismayed, for the Lord your God is with you wherever you go (Joshua 1:9).

Declarations

I pray now for the Presence of God to envelop and encompass you. In the presence of the God of love, fear cannot stay, because His perfect love drives out all fear. Thank you, Lord, for giving us a safe place to share our fears. We know that in Your presence is the fullness of joy.

1. We declare, as God has commanded, that we are strong and of good courage. We are not afraid or dismayed, for the Lord our God is with us wherever we go. (See Joshua 1:9.)
2. We declare God is love. There is no room in love for fear, so because God is with us, surrounding us, fear must be banished. (See 1 John 4:16,18.)
3. We declare that we have *no* fear of bad news; our hearts are steadfast, trusting in the Lord. Our hearts are secure, we will have no fear; in the end we will look in triumph on our foes. (See Psalm 112:7-8 NIV.)
4. We declare that we do not have a splintered mind. We *choose* to trust, and not to doubt God, and to believe! (See John 20:27.)
5. We declare that we listen to the wisdom of God, we dwell safely, and we are secure, without fear of evil. (See Proverbs 1:33.)
6. Thank you, Father God, that You will perfect and complete all that concerns me. (See Psalm 138:8.)
7. *Do not fear!* Thank you, Lord, for Your peace that surpasses knowledge. Wrap us all in Your perfect peace today.

Amen! Expect to be amazed!

Day 39
Men and Women of Strength

What is it to be a man or woman of strength? It is my hope that we will be strong in our God, without fear. In strength we put our trust in Him, and our expectancy on His plans for our lives, without the need to control.

I am strong when I release my cares to God; when I trust Him and remember that *all* things work together for good.

Loving God with all our heart makes us strong.

Receiving the joy of the Lord is our strength.

There is a difference between an inner strength that comes from trust in God, and fleshly efforts to be strong that build a wall around one's heart. Have you noticed strong women who have a hardness, and even a sharpness to them? It is like crusty, sharp calluses that develop from the erosion of their heart. Sometimes that woman I notice is me.

As judge and prophetess, Deborah was a leader with strength, but her strength came from her confidence in the Lord God Almighty. In the height of battle, she sang, "O my soul, March on in strength!" (See Judges 5:21.)

It is a verse I use often. Deborah also helped a man rise to victory in a critical battle. Without demeaning or criticizing Barak, she encouraged him to walk in the fullness of his strength.

Of course the Proverbs 31 woman was a woman of strength, both spiritually and physically.

Did you know the Bible encourages women to lift weights? *"She girds herself with strength and makes her arms strong and firm...She is clothed with strength and dignity, and she laughs without fear of the future"* (Proverbs 31:17-25 NIV).

I want to be styled in the beauty and elegance of the clothes of strength, dignity, and honor. It is feminine strength, the way God created us, and in my personal taste, a much better look than leathers with spikes.

Be strong in the Lord [be empowered through your union with Him]; Draw your strength from Him [that strength which His boundless might provides] (Ephesians 6:10 AMP).

Declarations

Father God, our Lord and Savior, I join my prayer with the other mighty men and women of God and we stand in agreement with Your Word, and Your promises. With the authority You have given us through Your Holy Spirit who dwells in us, we declare and decree the powerful Word of God:

1. We gird ourselves with strength! We declare we are clothed with strength and dignity, and we laugh without fear of the future. (See Proverbs 31:25.)
2. We declare the men and women You have appointed for Kingdom marriages have the strength to stick it out over the long haul—not the grim strength of gritting our teeth, but the glory-strength that endures the unendurable and spills over into joy. (See Colossians 1:11 MSG.)
3. And we thank the Father who makes us strong enough to take part in everything bright and beautiful that He has for us. (See Colossians 1:12 MSG.)
4. We declare blessings on ourselves and the people for whom we are praying, because our strength is in You. We have set our hearts on a pilgrimage, and we have passed through the Valley of Weeping. We receive Your rains that cover the dry places in our lives with pools of blessings. We go from strength to strength. (See Psalm 84:5-7.)
5. We declare over those for whom we are praying, "Be empowered through your union with Jesus Christ! Draw your strength from Him, that

strength which His boundless might provides." (See Ephesians 6:10 AMP.) And for ourselves we sing, "Oh my soul, march on in strength!" (See The Song of Deborah, Judges 5:21.)
6. We pray for the men called to Kingdom marriages, and we declare that they are men of strength. They are champions, heroes, warriors, mighty men; men of bravery.
7. I ask the God of our Master, Jesus Christ, the God of glory—to make us intelligent and discerning in knowing Him personally; our eyes focused and clear, so we can see exactly the utter extravagance of His work in us who trust Him—*endless energy, boundless strength*! (See Ephesians 1:15 MSG.)

Amen! Expect to be amazed!

Day 40
40 Days of Declarations

Thank you for walking with me through these 40 devotionals. My prayer for you is that your mind is renewed and your hope is restored. God is good, and He is 100 percent behind your desire for marriage.

Now go forth and overcome!

40 is the number of testing or trials.

40 Days it rained on Noah.

40 Days the land was flooded.

   The Dove returned with the olive branch – bringing hope and peace.

40 days Moses was on the mountain receiving revelation from God.

40 Days Joshua and Caleb and the other 10 spied out the Promised Land.

40 Years old was Caleb when he went to spy out the land with Joshua.

40 Years Joshua and Caleb believed, and waited.

40 Years the Israelites wandered in the wilderness.

40 Days Jesus fasted and was tested by Satan. The Holy Spirit came upon Jesus like a dove, empowering Him. Hope and peace.

40 Days Jesus appeared on the earth after the resurrection – and then He said,

> **"The Holy Spirit came upon Jesus like a dove**

DAY 40

"But you shall receive power when the Holy Spirit has come upon you, and you shall be witnesses to Me in Jerusalem, and in all Judea and Samaria, and to the end of the earth" (Acts 1:8).

40 Days of Declaring God's Word and His Promises!

Like Jesus when the enemy tested and tormented him, we have been declaring the powerful Word of God to speak truth over the lies. Truth is always victorious. Caleb and Joshua believed and waited for 40 years, which is a loooooong time to stand in faith, and to continue to declare the vision of hope and promise: The land flowing with milk and honey.

> Then Caleb quieted the people before Moses and said, "Let us go up at once and take possession for *we are well able to overcome it*" (Numbers 13:30).

Able: yakol, Strongs #3201. To be able, **to have power**, having the capacity to prevail or succeed.[1]

> "Caleb saw the same giants…but the 10 spies brought back an 'evil report' or unbelief [speaking words of unbelief]. Caleb's words declared a conviction – a 'confession' – before all Israel: 'We are well able to overcome.' He had surveyed the land, a reminder that faith is not blind. Faith does not deny the reality of difficulty, it declares the power of God in the face of the problem. Caleb's eventual possession of the land at a later date indicates that even though delays come, faith's confession will ultimately bring victory to the believer."[2]

My encouragement to all of us is do not give up! Do not back down or lose ground. Continue to wait with hope, and expect the victory in all areas of your life! We are well able to overcome anything! In the midst of delays, trials, and testing, continue to confess the faithfulness of God, and His Word. Continue to declare the promises, your desires, and dreams.

"You will prevail! Go out and do so" (1 Kings 22:22).

When the desire of your heart comes, it is the tree of life (Proverbs 13:12).

Declarations

Thank you, Lord, for Your Word and revelations these past 40 days. Thank you for imparting fresh hope to us; and thank you for filling us today with Your Holy Spirit who fills us with power. We celebrate You Lord! We rejoice in Your faithfulness! You are good!

1. We declare an impartation of the spirit of celebration to each person. And we receive Your joy! The joy of the Lord is our strength.
2. We declare the spirit of Caleb upon us all, to endure and believe, declaring faith in our good God. And when we declare, we receive power from the Holy Spirit.
3. We declare that "not a word will fail of any good thing which the Lord has spoken…all will come to pass." (See Joshua 21:45.)
4. We declare the Lord will answer us, and defend us! (See Psalm 20:1.)
5. We declare the Lord will grant us according to our heart's desire, and he will fulfill our purpose and destiny! (See Psalm 20:4.)
6. We declare that we will prevail, and as we set out and declare God's truth over discouragement, lies, and hopelessness, we will see transformation.
7. God is 100 percent behind my desire for marriage! He is good, and has the good gift of marriage for me and for the others for whom we are praying.

Be exalted oh Lord in Your own strength!

We sing and praise Your power! (Psalm 21:13)

Bless the Lord!

Amen! Expect to be amazed!

A Testimony from the Author

> It all works out for good in the end. So if it's not good, it's not the end!
> Kris Vallotton[1]

> And we know that all things work together for good to those who love God, to those who are the called according to His purpose (Romans 8:28).

My end-of-this-book testimony had been written and edited, all about the man I met at church, and our excitement for our future together. However, a few weeks before finalizing the manuscript for publishing, the promising romance ended. It was his decision, but as I distanced myself from the relationship, I realized I was striving to fix or ignore the issues of incompatibility. Our ten months together brought healing and strength to both of us, for which I am grateful.

Perhaps you have done this too. After waiting for Mr. Right, I wondered: *What's wrong with me? I won't give up this time. I will push through even though it seems more difficult than I think it should.*

As questions, doubts, disappointments and fear swirled in my mind, it was time to be alert and make choices of strength and courage…to see through the weighty fog, and focus on the One who brings light and clarity.

Unexpectedly, I have been invited to begin the journey of declarations again. These last few pages of the book are not the end of the story. Because of the 40 days of declaring God's truth, I am stronger and more hopeful than I was when I began chapter one. I pray that you are refreshed in hope, and quieted by His presence.

My faith is alive, my hope is in the God of Hope, and I *will* see the goodness of the Lord in the land of the living—for myself, and for you, too!

God is 100 percent behind my desire for marriage.

And He is the God of Romance!

I expect to be amazed!

And they lived happily ever after.

The Twelve Days of Christmas
Blessings for My Beloved

The first day of Christmas
Love

The Little Black Purse

The holiday season I moved my parents from a 4,200 square foot home into a 1,050 square foot apartment, I lost my connection with my "pray for marriages" blog. Feeling a bit like an ostrich with my head buried in the sand, I did not *feel* like praying for marriages, so I went into hiding with the excuse (and some truth) of getting buried in helping my parents move.

Going through the closets and looking through the collections of life was a process. I sorted and divided items for siblings, nieces, and nephews, and found old junk and a few timeless treasures. In the chaos of the clutter, I found a small, tired, and torn black purse, and I almost sent it to Goodwill without opening it first. I clicked the latch, opened it up, and inside was the greatest treasure! No, not my mother's lost ruby ring; not a $100 bill; but something far more valuable. Inside was a tiny piece of folded Christmas wrapping paper, tape intact, with these words lightly written on it:

> To my Darling Wife
>
> The Love of my life!
>
> All things are possible through Him who strengthens us.
>
> You can be all that you want to be!
>
> Love, David

What an extraordinary gift to me—a love note from my father to my mother.

Do not toss the treasures!

This Christmas season, remember to hold tightly to the promises God has given to you. I may not *feel* like praying, but I do believe that a good marriage is in God's plan for my life and your life, too.

Some of you wrestle as I do at Christmas time with the tension between the desires of your heart and reality. It is not just about marriage. The pain and struggles are numerous. *But God.* Christmas is a season of miracles, and we must remember that *all* things *are* possible!

Would you like to join me in praying 12 days of spiritual blessings for your beloved, known or unknown? If you are married, this is a great way to bless your spouse before Christmas Day.

If you are not married, there is someone out there waiting for *you*! They are aching for your gift of love, just as you are longing for them. We may not have our beloved yet to buy Christmas gifts for this year, but God knows who it is, and He wants to be our "UPS" man—**U**niting us by the **P**ower of the **S**pirit.

On the first day of Christmas, we give our true love... The gift of divine love.

Father God, together we pray that You surround our spouses (future or current) with Your perfect love that drives out all fear. Embrace our beloveds. Give them a new and greater experience of the love of Christ that surpasses knowledge. Help them comprehend what is the width, and length, and depth, and height of Your love for them. (See Ephesians 3:18.)

Fill them with Your heartbeat for the world around them; may Your love fill them and overflow to all who come in contact with them.

We pray and declare that we will love You, the Lord our God, with all of our hearts, with all of our souls, and with all of our minds.

And I must add a quote from my niece Elizabeth's blog, *Long to Love*:

When you pray, expect the immediate activity of God. Perhaps seen, likely unseen. Whatever it is in your life that pushes you to fall on your knees, to yearn and plead with God for supernatural intervention, pray for it and know He is moving. I love the Message version of Romans 8:26-28:

... the moment we get tired in the waiting, God's Spirit is right alongside helping us along. If we don't know how or what to pray, it doesn't matter. He does our praying in and for us, making prayer out of our wordless sighs, our aching groans. He knows us far better than we know ourselves; knows our pregnant condition; and keeps us present before God. That's why we can be so sure that every detail in our lives of love for God is worked into something good.[1]

We can know that God is moving in the life of someone we will embrace in the future—and He is Uniting us by the Power of His Holy Spirit!

Amen! Expect to be amazed!

The second day of Christmas
Peace

> **And suddenly there was with the angel a multitude of the heavenly host praising God and saying: "Glory to God in the highest, And on earth peace, goodwill toward men"** (Luke 2:13-14).

Can you even imagine what it would be like to suddenly see a multitude of the heavenly host praising God and declaring peace on Earth? Wow! The shepherds decided after the stunning and spectacular experience that it might be a good idea to go see baby Jesus.

> **Peace, shalom, Strong's #7965:** Completeness, wholeness, peace, health, welfare, safety, soundness, tranquility, prosperity, perfectness, fullness, rest, harmony, the absence of agitation of discord. Shalom comes from the root verb shalam, meaning "to be complete, perfect and full." Thus Shalom is much more than the absence of war and conflict; it is the wholeness the entire human race seeks.[2]

> Behold, on the mountains
>
> The feet of him who brings good tidings,
>
> Who proclaims peace!
>
> (Nahum 1:15)

Jesus came to bring peace; shalom. We enforce His peace by proclaiming *peace* wherever we go, and today we proclaim *peace* over the one we will marry, or have married. To help us understand the importance of praying declarative prayers in agreement with the Word of God, I share with you from the book *The Supernatural Ways of Royalty* by Kris Vallotton:

> We are partnering with God to bring justice to earth. (Peace!) Like Paul, we are restoring the knowledge of the one true God. Like Gideon, we are restoring the supernatural signs of God. We're restoring health to people's bodies, souls, and spirits. We're restoring relationships and families. We're restoring financial prosperity....
>
> The truth is that Christ defeated and disarmed the enemy once and for all on the Cross (see Col. 2:15). God has condemned him as guilty and handed over the authority he had usurped from Adam to Jesus Christ, the second Adam.
>
> Our job as "little Christs" is as deputies who enforce that judgment in every situation we come across. God created a world where our vote counts and where our agreement with all that He's doing is necessary to release His power into the world.[3]

**On the second day of Christmas, we give our true love…
The gift of peace!**

Our Father God, You are so amazing. Wonderful! Counselor! *Prince Of Peace!*

Thank you for delivering the enormous gift of peace today to the people You have Your hand on for a Kingdom marriage. Lord, bless the marriages of the people in our lives with shalom. (Add your own prayers to each definition of "shalom.")

We declare over our spouse:

Completeness in every area of their lives

Wholeness

Peace

Good health

Welfare

Safety

Soundness

Tranquility

Prosperity

Perfection

Wholeness

Rest

Harmony

The absence of agitation or discord

Lord, perfect and bring to completeness all that concerns them. (See Psalm 138:8.)

And I pray that each of us will have the mind of Christ to comprehend the power of our partnership with You, King of kings and Lord of lords.

Amen! Expect to be amazed!

The third day of Christmas
Kindness

> But what happens when we live God's way? He brings gifts into our lives, much the same way that fruit appears in an orchard—things like affection for others, exuberance about life, serenity. We develop a willingness to stick with things, a sense of compassion in the heart, and a conviction that a basic holiness permeates things and people. We find ourselves involved in loyal commitments, not needing to force our way in life, able to marshal and direct our energies wisely (Galatians 5:22-23 MSG).

As you may have guessed, the gifts we are sending via the Spirit to our spouse (future or current) are the fruits of the Spirit. Life is so much more pleasant when you and the people in your life are showing off their fruit of the Spirit!

> So I say, let the Holy Spirit guide your lives. Then you won't be doing what your sinful nature craves (Galatians 5:16 NLT).

> My counsel is this: Live freely, animated and motivated by God's Spirit. Then you won't feed the compulsions of selfishness (Galatians 5:16 MSG).

Selfishness – isn't that where relationships fall apart? Self-focus is a main cause of divorce, and when your eyes are always staring in a mirror, you will miss the person God has for you. Marriage is not just something we desire because it looks fun. Marriage is vital for the peace and wellbeing of society!

My hope and desire is that we will be filled afresh with the Holy Spirit daily, trusting God so completely the fruit of the Spirit is evident, and our self-absorption eradicated. The spiritual gifts we are sending to our beloveds are transformational! The powerful presence of God and the fruit of the Holy Spirit enable us to let go of fear, open our hearts to humanity, and *"live freely, animated and motivated by God's Spirit."* That freedom is irresistibly attractive!

> **Kindness. The Hebrew word is chrestotes, Strong's #5544: Goodness in action, sweetness of disposition, gentleness in dealing with others, benevolence, kindness, affability. The word describes the ability to act for the welfare of those taxing your patience. The Holy Spirit removes abrasive qualities from the character of one under His control.**[4]

I want that! And I would like my future husband to be a genuinely kind person.

> **On the third day of Christmas, we give our true love...**
> **The gift of Kindness.**

Gracious God, You are so kind. This Christmas, and right now, fill our spouse with Your Holy Spirit—so full, they fall more deeply in love with You, letting go of fear and the cares of the world. As they are filled with Your Spirit, give them an extra measure of kindness, so they will:

Exhibit goodness in action;

Have sweetness of disposition;

Be gentle when dealing with others;

Live a life of benevolence;

Be friendly, approachable and kind to others.

Thank you, Lord, for Your faithfulness! Thank you for transforming us more each day by the renewing of our minds through Your powerful Word. Thank you for bringing our beloved closer to us every day. Thank you Holy **UPS** man, for **U**niting us by the **P**ower of Your **S**pirit!

> **Amen! Expect to be amazed!**

The fourth day of Christmas
Joy

But the angel said to them, "Do not be afraid; for behold, I bring you good news of a great joy, which will come to all the people" (Luke 2:10 AMP).

Jesus is *the* great joy! Even though your life might not look the way you had hoped and dreamed this Christmas, receive and be filled with the greatest joy! And join me in praying that angels deliver the message of great joy to your spouses, future spouses, and families.

Though the fig tree may not blossom, nor fruit be on the vines; though the labor of the olive may fail, and the fields yield no food; though the flock may be cut off from the fold; And there be no herd in the stalls; yet I will rejoice in the Lord. I will joy in the God of my salvation. The Lord God is my strength. He will make my feet like deer's feet; and He will make me walk on my high hills (Or high heels!) (Habakkuk 3:17-19).

He will! Thank you, Lord!

Joy gil (geel), Strong's #1523: To joy, rejoice, be glad, be joyful. Gil contains the suggestion of "dancing for joy," or "leaping for joy," since the verb originally meant "to spin around with intense motion." Although everything is wrong in Habakkuk's external world, he is leaping for joy over his fellowship with Yahweh.[5]

Do not sorrow, for the joy of the Lord is your strength (Nehemiah 8:10).

On the fourth day of Christmas, I give my true love…joy!

Father God, we pray and declare that You are imparting to our spouse, future or current, unspeakable *joy*! Be our **UPS** Man, and **U**nite us *in joy* by the **P**ower of Your **S**pirit.

- Despite their circumstances and busyness, give them feet like deer that they can walk on the high hills and overcome anything pulling them into discouragement.

- We declare (from Song of Solomon 2:17) turn my beloved! And be like a gazelle, or a young stag, and leap over the mountain of Bether (separation).

- Fill them with Your Holy Spirit today, so full that they cannot contain the joy! Impart to them leaping, spin-around *joy*; contagious *joy*!

- And sensitize their spirits. Give them a childlike spirit, expectant for Christmas morning. A spirit that will leap for joy when their spouse (future or current) walks into the room like John the Baptist leapt in Elizabeth's womb. (See Luke 1:41.)

- Lord, impart to them the *joy* and *gladness* in You, that will strengthen them until we are **U**nited, face to face, by the **P**ower of Your **S**pirit!

Amen! Expect to be amazed!

The fifth day of Christmas
Patience

The other word for patience is LOOOOOOOOOOOOOONG-Suffering. When is long suffering, too-long-suffering? God is right on time, though I must say, it seems as though His timing is delayed when it's *not* according to *my* microwave timing.

Abraham and Sarah must have felt that God's timing for the fulfillment of God's promise for a child was a bit too long, too. And what about the Israelites who waited 400 years in spiritual darkness before Jesus broke through with His glorious light? They must have struggled with patience, and that was indeed long-suffering.

> **Patience, makrothumia; Strong's #3115: From makros, "long," and thurmos, "temper." The word denotes leniency, forbearance, fortitude, patient endurance, and long-suffering. Also included in makrothumia is the ability to endure persecution and ill treatment. It describes a person who has the power to exercise revenge, but instead exercises restraint. This quality is a fruit of the Spirit.**[6]

God is patient with us, and when we abide in His Spirit, we have His supernatural gift of patience.

> **I waited and waited and waited for God. At last He looked; finally He listened (Psalm 40:1 MSG).**

> **And we desire that each one of you show the same diligence to the full assurance of hope until the end, that you do not become sluggish,**

but imitate those who through faith and patience inherit the promises (Hebrews 6:11-12).

**On the fifth day of Christmas, we give our true love...
The gift of patience.**

Patient God, we pray for our future (or existing) spouses, that You will deliver to them an extra measure of patience and long-suffering by Your Spirit:

- That they will be lenient with others;

- Exercise restraint when provoked;

- Have fortitude and patient endurance.

Just as we have been waiting and waiting and waiting, the other person has been waiting too.

> **Now may the God of patience and comfort grant you to be likeminded toward one another, according to Christ Jesus, that you with one mind and one mouth glorify the God and Father of our Lord Jesus Christ (Romans 15:5).**

Thank you, Lord, for sending the Comforter to them while they wait with patience for us! Thank you **UPS** Man, for **U**niting us by the **P**ower of Your Holy **S**pirit!

Amen! Expect to be amazed!

The sixth day of Christmas
Goodness

One of the things I hear in circles of unmarried people is, "all the *good* ones are taken."

Or, "there aren't any *good* guys out there (in the dating world)."

I cringe when I hear people say things like that! Our words have power, and if we *say* "the good ones are gone," it will be more challenging to *see* the great ones when God brings them into our lives. I admit, sometimes it seems that all the good guys are married, but I am careful not to agree with such faithless words.

God is *good*, and He is more than "able to do exceedingly abundantly above *all* that we ask or think, according to the power that works in *us*!" (See Ephesians 3:20.)

There are good men and women, just like you, waiting to find their beloved. So when you start feeling discouragement weigh you down like a wet blanket, whispering lies to your mind, speak the truth—the powerful Word of God over the lies.

> Now I myself am confident concerning you, my brethren, that you also are full of *goodness*, filled with all knowledge, able also to admonish one another (Romans 15:14).
>
> Goodness, agathosune; Strong's #19: Compare "Agatha", and possibly "agate." Beneficence, kindness in actual manifestation, virtue equipped for action, a bountiful propensity both to will and to do

what is good, intrinsic goodness producing a generosity and a Godlike state of being. Agathosune is a rare word that combines being good and doing good.[7]

The other day I was feeling the expectancy of God's blessings in my life, grateful for the things I have yet to see, and I felt Him say to my heart. *"I am blessing you not because you are good, but because I Am good."*

Some days the only thing I can pray is, "God, I know You are good, and You are faithful." When we focus on His goodness and love for us, then goodness will be a result of His Spirit living in us. Fruit of the Spirit! It doesn't happen from striving to do all the right or "good" things so we will *get* what we want. He is not Santa Claus. Whether we are naughty or nice, God is still good.

One of the pastors from my church, Simon, says, "when you need something in your life, give it away, and God will give it to you in greater measure." We could all use more goodness, so let's give some away!

On the sixth day of Christmas, we give our true love... The gift of goodness.

God, You are *good*! Thank you for Your goodness in our lives. Thank you that because you are *good*, You will hear our prayers and touch the lives of people we may or may not even know today—our future or current spouses!

- Fill them today with Your Holy Spirit. Compel them to ask You to fill them today.

- Fill our spouses with Your goodness!

- Fill them with Your virtue that is equipped for action.

- Impart to the people You have called to Kingdom marriages a bountiful propensity both to will and to do what is good.

- Generous God, fill them with Your generosity.

- Give them the strength to be good and to do good and fill them with the knowledge to know it is because You are good.

We declare there are *great* people "out there" in the dating world, and we know that God is our Matchmaker!

> **Indeed I have spoken it; I will also bring it to pass. I have purposed it; I will also do it (God)—(Isaiah 46:11).**
>
> **Amen! Expect to be amazed!**

The seventh day of Christmas
Faithfulness

A faithful man will abound with blessings… (Proverbs 28:20).

One Christmas, I was looking at an impossible situation. While trying to have enough faith to believe that God would come through for me, my prayer shifted. I began asking God to increase my faith and strengthen me to believe that He will do what He says He will do. I realized that I could not muster up enough faith by my own striving; it had to come from God. It's the picture of letting go, falling back, and trusting that He will be there to catch you. He always does, because our awesome God is faithful! So faithful!

God did come through for me in the situation that seemed impossible.

I want to be full of faith every day. It is my desire to meet a man who is so full of faith that he is unwaveringly faithful to me, after he is steadfastly faithful to God.

> **Faithful, emunah; Strong's #530:** Firmness, stability, faithfulness, fidelity, conscientiousness, steadiness, certainty; that which is permanent, enduring, steadfast. Emunah comes from the root "a man," to be firm, sure, established and steady. "Amen" derived from this same root, means "it is firmly, truly so!" Emunah is often translated "faithfulness" or "truth," as truth is considered something ultimately certain, stable, and unchangingly fixed.[8]

God is firm—He doesn't move or change His mind. We are created in the image of God. We are filled and empowered by His indwelling Holy Spirit so we can ask for more of His attributes in our own lives, and for the life of our beloved.

On the seventh day of Christmas, we give our true love... The gift of faithfulness.

Thank you, Father God, for Your firm faithfulness! You are so faithful to Your promises; and to complete what You began in our lives. You invited us on this journey to pray for Kingdom marriages, and I believe that all of us will receive the desires of our hearts—Your best marriages. Lord, help our unbelief, and give us the gift of faith to believe the unbelievable, and to wait with hope and expectancy.

Lord God, fill our (future or current) beloved with Your Holy Spirit; fill them with the gift of *faith*, that they will bear much fruit of faithfulness.

- Impart to our beloved the miraculous faith of Mary and Joseph this Christmas.

- Increase their faith to believe that You adore them, and that You will bless them with a great romance.

- Make their faithfulness firm, so they will be:

Loyal

Constant

Dedicated

Devoted

Devout

Staunch

Steadfast

Resolute

- And we declare the faithful men and women You have called to unite in Kingdom marriages will abound with blessings.

Thank you, **UPS** Man, for **U**niting us by the **P**ower of Your **S**pirit!

Amen! It is firmly, truly so.

Expect to be amazed!

The eighth day of Christmas
Gentleness

Producing the fruit of the Spirit in our lives is relatively easy when we are around other lovely, fruit-bearing people. The challenge to be loving, kind, and gentle comes when we are confronted by the unlovely people who are not kind or courteous, or who speak harshly to us. Have you noticed how aggressive drivers are during Christmas? Or is it just Colorado? My fruit tends to wilt when I am cut off, or the other driver forgets to alternate.

I heard from a man-friend while he was visiting his parents for Christmas. He was trying to love an unlovely father—a father who has not blessed, but has been mean and demeaning to his only son. It is much more challenging to produce the fruit of gentleness or meekness when the attacks from others come.

> Come to Me, all you who labor and are heavy-laden and overburdened, and I will cause you to rest. [I will ease and relieve and refresh your souls.] Take My yoke upon you and learn of Me, for I am *gentle* (meek) and humble (lowly) in heart, and you will find rest (relief and ease and refreshment and recreation and blessed quiet) for your souls. For My yoke is wholesome (useful, good not harsh, hard, sharp, or pressing, but comfortable, gracious and pleasant), and My burden is light and easy to be borne (Matthew 11:28-30, AMP).

> Gentleness, praotes; Strong's #4236: A disposition that is even-tempered, tranquil, balanced in spirit, unpretentious, and that has the passions under control. The word is best translated "meekness," not as an indication of weakness, but of power and strength under control. The person who possesses this quality pardons injuries, corrects faults, and rules his own spirit well.[9]

Jesus entered our world as the most humble, meek and gentle being we can imagine; an innocent baby, born in the mess and cold of a manger. Nothing is impossible with God. Jesus modeled the power of gentleness. He did not react, as we would like to, when he was rejected, or beaten, or cut off in line while trying to buy a gift. When He stood in love and gentleness, He used the most powerful and effective retaliation of all. Gentleness is warfare when it needs to be, and the fruit of the Holy Spirit of the most awesome God is powerful!

We are mighty when we are yoked with Jesus; not striving to be or do all the right things in our own strength or cleverness. We need *His* strength, wisdom, love, and power.

> **On the eighth day of Christmas, we give our true love...**
> **The gift of gentleness.**

Thank you, Jesus, for demonstrating the true meaning of gentleness and meekness. Thank you for the supernatural power of the fruit of Your Spirit! Fill us afresh with Your Holy Spirit today, and fill those who are called to join us in Kingdom marriages.

Holy Spirit, fill us, and fill our true loves with Your fruit of gentleness, meekness and humility; for when we are filled and inflated with Your Spirit, we cannot be inflated with pride.

Give us both Your quiet strength, and empower us today.

We declare gentleness to be imparted by the Holy Spirit to us and to them, that we will have a disposition that is even-tempered, tranquil, balanced in spirit, unpretentious, and has passion under control. We will pardon injuries, correct faults, and rule our own spirits well.

Father God, cause us to remove the yoke of heaviness, and to take Your yoke upon us, that we will find rest—relief and ease and refreshment and recreation and blessed quiet—for our souls.

Thank you God, that You are the great restorer. Bring Your restoration in these miraculous days of Christmas.

Amen! Expect to be amazed!

The ninth day of Christmas
Prosperity

One of the issues I have heard and observed from the men is their need to feel financially stable before they commit to a long-term relationship or marriage. Women desire security, and it is better to begin a marriage when debt is managed.

> Save now, I pray, O Lord; O Lord, I pray, send now prosperity (Psalm 118:25).

> Let the Lord be magnified, Who has pleasure in the prosperity of His servant (Psalm 35:27).

We know the words we speak or pray or declare have the power to change and create because we are sons and daughters of the King of kings! We have dominion! This Christmas, let's send a blessing of *prosperity to* the person God has chosen as our Kingdom marriage partner (future or current marriage).

One of the Hebrew words for prosper or prosperity is shalom – peace!

> **Prosper, tsalach; Strong's #6743:** To rush; to advance, prosper, make progress, succeed, be profitable. To make prosperous, bring to successful issue, cause to prosper. To show or experience prosperity, prosper.[10]

This is an interesting word because tsalach is the same word used when the Holy Spirit came upon David, Saul, and Gideon to empower them for victory. Come upon us, Holy Spirit, that we may succeed in the work and works You have given us to accomplish.

**On the ninth day of Christmas, we give our true love...
The gift of prosperity.**

Father God, thank you for sending Your anointing to prosper to the people You have chosen to join us in Kingdom marriages. Thank you that when we declare Your word, which is *the* truth, changes will happen in the lives of the people for whom we are praying—even though we may not know them yet.

Lord God, we declare a multiplication of Your Word to change the atmosphere, and to change mindsets!

Holy Spirit, we pray, come upon (prosper) the people You have called to Kingdom marriage. Send prosperity *now!*

Give them shalom—*peace* and prosperity.

We declare that our spouses "will remember the Lord their God, **for it is He who gives you the power to get wealth**, that He may establish His covenant which He swore to your fathers" *(Deuteronomy 8:18).*

We declare that, "He *(our spouse)* will be like a tree planted by rivers of water, that brings forth fruit in its season, whose leaf shall not wither; **and whatever he does shall prosper!**" *(See Psalm 1:3.)*

Thank you, Lord, that we can hope, and wait with expectancy for the fulfillment of the desires of our hearts.

Amen! It is firmly, truly so!

> **Expect to be amazed!**

The tenth day of Christmas
Discernment

Every day that I was subscribed to Match. com, I would receive an email with a selection of men they had chosen for me on a particular day. It is sort of like the "Shop It To Me" emails I receive with all the great designer fashions that are on sale, based on my preselected criteria. It's all shopping. Anyway, the nice looking photo labeled, "Sagacious Gentleman" caught my eye, not as much because of the way he looked, or that he is a big skier—no, it was the word "sagacious." I must confess, I had to look up the word, and I am glad I did.

Sagacious:

- Keen in sense perception.

- Of keen and farsighted penetration and judgment: discerning.

- Caused by or indicating acute discernment.

- Synonyms: discerning, insightful, perceptive, prudent, wise, sage, sapient.

The "sagacious gentleman" was looking for a woman with "acute discernment and a keen practical sense."

Discernment is a much more valuable trait to look for in a person than "a woman who can look equally great in a little black dress or jeans," (a popular criteria on Match. com).

My friend, mentor, and spiritual father, Ed Silvoso, in his incredible book, *Women, God's Secret Weapon*, shares this important revelation:

> **In the same fashion that men are to protect women's minds, women are designed to protect men's hearts.**

The expression "suitable help" used by God to describe Eve in ancient Hebrew means "the revealer of the enemy." Eve proved this when she identified Satan as the deceiver.[11]

The discerning of spirits is one of the gifts of the Holy Spirit, and one I would like to send via **UPS** to the man God is leading to me day by day.

On the tenth day of Christmas, we give our true love… The gift of discernment.

Thank you, Father God, for the sagacious ladies and gentlemen You are preparing for each of us, and for Kingdom marriages. Please **U**nite us by the **P**ower of Your **S**pirit, and send them an increase of the supernatural gifts of discernment and wisdom.

Just as the wise men could read the stars, and knew a King was born, give our spouses the wisdom needed to know the next steps in their journey.

Give them spiritual and natural eyes to see, and ears to hear Your voice saying to them, "this is the way, walk in it."

Impart to each person sensitivity in their spirit, to know Your best when presented with a choice.

For you (my beloved) have not been given a spirit of fear, but of love, power, and a sound mind (see 2 Timothy 1:7).

> **Sound mind, sophronisomos; Strong's #4995: The word denotes good judgment, disciplined thought patterns, and the ability to understand and make right decisions. It includes the qualities of self-control and self-discipline.[12]**

Give our beloveds an increase of Your wisdom, and the good sense to ask You for wisdom daily.

Give our beloveds the mind of Christ, to know their true identity as the King's heir, child, and loved one.

Thank you, dear Lord, for the anticipation we feel today; the expectancy, and hope. Thank you, Jesus, for hope.

Amen! It is firmly, truly so!

Expect to be amazed!

The eleventh day of Christmas
Awe and Wonder and the fear of the Lord

Every Christmas, my sister Jennifer and her family host a fabulous Christmas party for her family and close friends. I must confess that most years anticipating the party was a little bit stressful for me, because I hope and pray that I will finally have *the* date to the big party. I usually choose to go solo, and I always have a great time catching up with the festive people I see just once a year.

After much unnecessary angst and over-analyzing, I asked a man-friend to join me at the party one year. Why was it so stressful for me? Was I worried about what people would think if I showed up solo...again? Every year, a generation of 15+ years younger than me arrives with spouses and children, and I enjoy them all, while stuffing my "hope deferred." Worrying about appearances is "fearing" man rather than trusting God. I don't think man-fearing was the main reason for my angst, it was a bit deeper. I realized that my resistance in asking a friend was rooted in my desire to enjoy *all* of Christmas with my true love. I don't want just *a* date; I long for *the* date.

So this year, I pray—*we* pray—for the man or woman God is preparing for us, and we pray for the many other people longing for a Kingdom marriage. May we have a deeply rooted awe, wonder, and reverence for the Son of God; that is the "fear of the Lord."

> **The Lord of hosts—regard Him as holy and honor His holy name [by regarding Him as your only hope of safety], and let Him be your fear and let Him be your dread [lest you offend Him by your fear of man and distrust of Him] (Isaiah 8:13 AMP).**

Fear morah, Strong's #4172: Fear, reverence, terror, awe; an object of fear, respect, or reverence…. In the reference, Isaiah is admonished never to fear human threats, but to let God alone be the object of his reverential fear.[13]

> **On the eleventh day of Christmas, we give our true love… awe, wonder, and the fear of the Lord.**

Wonderful, Counselor, Mighty God, Everlasting Father, Prince of Peace—we declare that we honor and revere You. We worship You! We are in awe of You, and we open our hearts and spirits to receive Your majesty and the wonder of all that You are.

Give our true loves, and all who are appointed for Kingdom marriages, the gift of a deep fear of You—a gasping wonder and awe when we think of You and feel Your presence. We trade in our fear of man, and choose to fear the Lord.

Amen! Expect to be amazed!

Merry Christmas
Life and Light

> And suddenly there was with the angel a multitude of heavenly host praising God, and saying, "Glory to God in the highest, And on earth peace, goodwill toward men!"
>
> (Luke 2:13-14)

**On the twelfth day of Christmas, we give our true love…
The gift of life and light.**

Glory to God in the highest. Thank you, Lord, that we can celebrate today the miraculous birth of Jesus Christ.

Jesus, please invade the lives of those who are called to join us in Kingdom marriage. Break into their hearts, and into their lives in a new, miraculous way.

We speak *new divine life and light* to the dreams that have died, and pray for new dreams to be given and imparted to their spirits, minds, and hearts today.

We speak *new divine life and light* to all areas needing the Light of the World to expose doors that need to be closed, and shine on new doors that are ready to be opened.

Give them the keys to the Kingdom on this Christmas Day.

Fill them with more of You, Jesus, today.

Give them new gifts of Your divine hope, joy, peace, and Your perfect love.

EXPECT TO BE AMAZED!

Give them the expectancy of a child this Christmas morning, and eyes to see clearly Your *best* gift for them.

And thank you, great God, for all of Your gifts today, and that next year many of us praying today will be with our true love for Christmas!

Amen! It is firmly, truly so!

Expect to be amazed!

Appendix A
Who I Am in Christ

- I am the apple of God's eye, and I am hidden under the shadow of His wings (Psalm 17:8).
- I am my Beloved's and He is mine (Song of Solomon 6:3).
- I am beautiful – created in the image of God (Genesis 1:27).
- I am far from oppression, and fear does not come near me (Isaiah 54:14).
- I am born of God, and the evil one does not touch me (1 John 5:18).
- I have the mind of Christ (1 Corinthians 2:16; Philippians 2:5).
- I have the peace of God that passes all understanding (Philippians 4:7).
- I have the Greater One living in me; greater is He Who is in me than he who is in the world (1 John 4:4).
- I can quench all the fiery darts of the wicked one with my shield of faith (Ephesians 6:16).
- I can do all things through Christ Jesus who strengthens me (Philippians 4:13).
- I am God's workmanship, created in Christ unto good works (Ephesians 2:10).
- I am a believer, and the light of the Gospel shines in my mind (2 Corinthians 4:4).
- I am a child of God and a joint-heir with Christ (Romans 8:17).
- I am more than a conqueror through Him Who loves me (Romans 8:37).
- I am an overcomer by the blood of the Lamb and the word of my testimony (Revelation 12:11).
- I am part of a chosen generation, a royal priesthood, a holy nation, a purchased people (1 Peter 2:9).
- I am the righteousness of God in Jesus Christ (2 Corinthians 5:21).

- I am the head and not the tail; I am above only and not beneath (Deuteronomy 28:13).
- I am His elect, full of mercy, kindness, humility, and longsuffering (Romans 8:33; Colossians 3:12).
- I am forgiven of all my sins and washed in the Blood (Ephesians 1:7).
- I am redeemed from the curse of sin, sickness, and poverty (Deuteronomy 28:15- 68; Galatians 3:13).
- I am healed by the stripes of Jesus (Isaiah 53:5; 1 Peter 2:24).
- I am greatly loved by God (Romans 1:7; Ephesians 2:4; Colossians 3:12; 1 Thessalonians 1:4).
- I am strengthened with all might according to His glorious power (Colossians 1:11).
- I am submitted to God, and the devil flees from me because I resist him in the Name of Jesus (James 4:7).
- I press on toward the goal to win the prize to which God in Christ Jesus is calling us upward (Philippians 3:14).
- For God has not given us a spirit of fear; but of power, love, and a sound mind (2 Timothy 1:7).
- It is not I who live, but Christ lives in me (Galatians 2:20).

Appendix B

The Right Reverend and Right Honorable Dr. Richard Chartres KCVO, Bishop of London, gave the following address at the marriage of HRH Prince William of Wales to Miss Catherine Middleton at Westminster Abbey.[1]

"Be who God meant you to be and you will set the world on fire." So said St. Catherine of Siena whose festival day this is. Marriage is intended to be a way in which man and woman help each other to become what God meant each one to be, their deepest and their truest selves.

Many people are fearful for the future of today's world, but the message of the celebrations in this country and far beyond its shores is the right one—this is a joyful day! It is good that people on every continent are able to share in these celebrations because this is, as every wedding day should be, a day of hope.

In a sense every wedding is a royal wedding with the bride and groom as king and queen of creation, making a new life together so that life can flow through them into the future.

William and Catherine, you have chosen to be married in the sight of a generous God who so loved the world that he gave himself to us in the person of Jesus Christ. In the Spirit of this generous God, husband and wife are to give themselves to each other.

The spiritual life grows as love finds its center beyond ourselves. Faithful and committed relationships offer a door into the mystery of spiritual life in which we discover this: the more we give of self, the richer we become in soul; the more we go beyond ourselves in love, the more we become our true selves and our spiritual beauty is more fully revealed. In marriage we are seeking to bring one another into fuller life.

It is of course very hard to wean ourselves away from self-centeredness. People can dream of such a thing but that hope should not be fulfilled without a solemn decision that, whatever the difficulties, we are committed to the way of generous love.

You have both made your decision today—"I will"—and by making this new relationship, you have aligned yourselves with what we believe is the way in which life is spiritually evolving, and which will lead to a creative future for the human race.

We stand looking forward to a century which is full of promise and full of peril. Human beings are confronting the question of how to use wisely the power that has been given to us through the discoveries of the last century. We shall not be converted to the promise of the future by more knowledge, but rather by an increase of loving wisdom and reverence, for life, for the earth and for one another.

Marriage should transform, as husband and wife make one another their work of art. It is possible to transform so long as we do not harbor ambitions to reform our partner. There must be no coercion if the Spirit is to flow; each must give the other space and freedom. Chaucer, the London poet, sums it up in a pithy phrase:

> **"Whan maistrie [mastery] comth, the God of Love anon, Beteth his wynges, and farewell, he is gon."**

As the reality of God has faded from so many lives in the West, there has been a corresponding inflation of expectations that personal relations alone will supply meaning and happiness in life. This is to load our partner with too great a burden. We are all incomplete: we all need the love which is secure, rather than oppressive. We need mutual forgiveness in order to thrive.

As we move towards our partner in love, following the example of Jesus Christ, the Holy Spirit is quickened within us and can increasingly fill our lives with light. This leads on to a family life which offers the best conditions in which the next generation can receive and exchange those gifts which can overcome fear and division and incubate the coming world of the Spirit, whose fruits are love and joy and peace.

I pray that all of us present and the many millions watching this ceremony and sharing in your joy today will do everything in their power to support and uphold you in your new life. I pray that God will bless you in the way of life you have chosen. That way which is expressed in the prayer that you have composed together in preparation for this day:

God our Father, we thank you for our families; for the love that we share and for the joy of our marriage.

In the busyness of each day keep our eyes fixed on what is real and important in life and help us to be generous with our time and love and energy.

Strengthened by our union, help us to serve and comfort those who suffer. We ask this in the Spirit of Jesus Christ.

Amen.

Appendix C
Soul Ties Keys for Prayer Ministers: Cutting Yourself Free from Unholy Unions
by Norma Dearing[1]

> Or do you not know that the one who joins himself to a harlot is one body with her? For He says, the two will become one flesh (1 Corinthians 6:16).

If we think in terms of being "connected" to all the people in the past with whom we have had intimate relations, (many before knowing Jesus), it is overwhelming to contemplate. Many of these connections were very unhealthy, perhaps even when we were under the influence of drugs or alcohol. Many people have told me they were so sexually active in their college days or military lives that they can't even remember all the people. In these cases, we pray a general prayer trusting that the Lord remembers and will cut them free.

When two people join physically, spiritually, and emotionally, outside of marriage the two become one flesh in unholy union. Their spirits reach out and connect with one another. The connections that are made bring spiritual confusion and spiritual ties.

These ties will remain until they are broken. I firmly believe this is something that should be done with every couple during premarital counseling. A marriage entered where the couple can be united in oneness with each other and Jesus is one with the best future. In cases of divorce or death, this includes being cut free from previous spouses before remarriage. When

APPENDIX C

this seems unusually difficult for a person, it may be a sign they are not yet ready to release a prior relationship and to be totally connected to another in marriage.

Other instances where a person needs to be cut free from a sexual partner in body, mind and spirit include when he or she is not a willing participant in the sexual act, as in cases of rape, incest, or sexual abuse. Tremendous healing takes place when we pray with clients in this area. There probably is still a need for healing of the memories, but this often opens the door for inner healing.

Following is a very simple prayer you may want to pray for yourself or with a prayer partner:

In the name of Jesus Christ and by the power of His cross and blood, we take the sword of the Spirit and cut _____ free from all previous sexual partners. We especially cut _____ free from _____, _____, _____, _____ (first names or initials only). We cut him/her free from these people physically, spiritually, emotionally and mentally. We not only cut him/her free from these people, Lord, but also from anyone and everyone with whom those people have ever had sexual relations. We place the cross and the blood of Jesus between _____ and each of these people. We pray for a cleansing and purification of _____'s mind, body and spirit; that he/she may walk in wholeness, purification and redemption. Fill _____ with the power of Your Holy Spirit, that he/she may walk in Your abundant grace and mercy. Fill him/her, Lord, with Your love, that it may permeate all dark and lonely places. Most of all, Lord, help _____ to know how much You love him/her and how special he/she is to You.

End Notes

Introduction

1. Arthur Burke, Releasing Singles Audio CD (Anaheim, CA: Plumbline Ministries, 2005). Out of print.
2. Patricia King, Finding Your Mate DVD (Maricopa, AZ: XP Publishing, 2014). http://store. xpministries. com/products/finding-mate-dvd?variant=635641341.
3. Patricia King, Finding Your Mate DVD (Maricopa, AZ: XP Publishing, 2014). http://store. xpministries. com/products/finding-mate-dvd?variant=635641341.
4. Charles Capps, Faith and Confession (England, AR: Capps Publishing, 1987) page 29.
5. Steve Backlund, Igniting Hope Ministries, http://ignitinghope.com/blog/how-i-started-making-declarations.
6. Kris Vallotton, The Supernatural Ways of Royalty (Shippensburg, PA: Destiny Image, 2006) page 70.
7. Patricia King, 10 Keys to Success (Maricopa, AZ: XP Publishing, 2013) page 24.
8. James Goll – Facebook post: https://www.facebook.com/jamesgollpage/photos/a.394458211831.170987.146839486831/10152521135006832/.
9. John Maxwell, The Power of Thinking Big (Tulsa, OK: River Oak Publishing, 2001) introduction page.
10. Jeff Olsen, The Slight Edge (Lake Dallas, TX: Success Books, 2005) page 158.
11. Charles Capps, Faith and Confession (England, AR: Capps Publishing, 1987) page 183.

Day 1

1. Cindy Jacobs, Women of Destiny (Ventura, CA, Regal Books, 1998) page 150.
2. Note on Genesis 1:26, New Spirit Filled Life Bible (Nashville, TN, Thomas Nelson, Inc., 2002) page 5.

Day 2

1. Author Unknown, Man with a Mop blog, http://man-with-the-mop.blogspot.com/2006/11/kingdom-marriage-to-have-and-to-hold. html.

END NOTES

Day 4

1. Francis Frangipane, Your Appointment with Your Destiny is Still Set, The Elijah List, September 27, 2010, http://www.elijahlist.com/words/display_word.html?ID=9171
2. Frangipane, Your Appointment with Destiny is Still Set,

Day 5

1. Hope, Word Wealth, New Spirit Filled Life Bible (Nashville, TN, Thomas Nelson, Inc., 2002) page 1146.
2. Bob Hazlett, FaceBook quote: https://www.facebook.com/bobhazlett.org/photos/a.339924912744686.77700.320085828061928/708623359208171/.

Day 6

1. Kris Vallotton, Hope The Divine X Factor audio message, February 6, 2013. http://www.kvministries.com/podcast/2013/02/06/hope-divine-x-factor.

Day 7

1. Charles Capps, Faith and Confession (England, AR:Capps Publishing, 1987) page 52.

Day 8

1. India Arie, Strength Courage and Wisdom, Universal Motown Records, March 27, 2001.
2. Strong's Concordance – #2470

Day 9

1. Strong's concordance, #H909
2. Doug Addison, Divine Alliances (Santa Maria, CA: In Light Connection, 2009) pages 7, 23.

Day 10

1. Stacie and John Eldredge, Captivating (Nashville, TN: Thomas Nelson Inc., 2005) page 13.
2. Eldredge, *Captivating*, 100-101
3. Eldredge, *Captivating*, 101

Day 11

1. Garris Elkins, Desires and dreams of the heart, February 11, 2012 Elijah List.

END NOTES

Day 13

1. Bob Hartley with Michael Sullivant, The Hope Reformation, Four Hopes and Four Snakes, April 4, 2013, http://bobhartley.org/4-4-13-our-latest-elijah-list-article-4-hopes-and-4-snakes/.

Day 14

1. Endures, Word Wealth, New Spirit Filled Life Bible (Nashville, TN, Thomas Nelson, Inc., 2002) page 1335.

Day 15

1. Rob Bell, Sex God: Exploring the Endless Connections between Sexuality and Spirituality (Grand Rapids, MI: Harper Collins 2007) pages 148-150.
2. Bob Hazlett Facebook post; https://www.facebook.com/bobhazlett.org/posts/522003731203469.
3. Note for Ruth 3:9, New Spirit Filled Life Bible (Nashville, TN, Thomas Nelson, Inc., 2002) page 356. Middle Eastern world involved the practice of the casting of a garment over one being claimed for marriage.

Day 16

1. Man, Word Wealth, New Spirit Filled Life Bible (Nashville, TN, Thomas Nelson, Inc., 2002) page 1003.
2. http://www.chabad.org/library/article_cdo/aid/477334/jewish/The-Procession.htm.

Day 18

1. Ann Voskamp, Figuring Out How to Forgive Your Parents, A Holy Experience blog, August 10, 2011, http://www.aholyexperience.com/2011/08/figuring-out-how-to-forgive-your-parents/.

Day 20

1. Doug Addison, Divine Alliances (Santa Maria, CA: In Light Connection, 2009) page 18.

Day 21

1. Alison Armstrong, Making Sense of Men (Sherman Oaks, CA: Pax Programs, 2007) pages 47-50.

Day 23

1. Patricia King, The Favor Factor (Maricopa, AZ: XP Ministries, 2013) page 11.

END NOTES

Day 24

1. Be Strong, Word Wealth, New Spirit Filled Life Bible (Nashville, TN, Thomas Nelson Inc., 2002) page 279.

Day 26

1. James Robison, The Holy Spirit and Restoration, New Spirit Filled Life Bible,
2. Derek Prince (Nashville, TN, Thomas Nelson Inc., 2002) page, 279 God is a Matchmaker (Grand Rapids, MI, Chosen Books, 1986) page 20.

Day 27

1. Christopher West, The Theology of the Body for Beginners (West Chester, PA, Ascension Press, 2004, 2009) page 31 -51.
2. West, The Theology of the Body for Beginners, 31-51.
3. West, The Theology of the Body for Beginners, 31-51

Day 28

1. Arthur Burke's website, www.theslg.com, and Releasing Singles maybe found on Amazon.com.

Day 29

1. Derek Prince, God is a Matchmaker (Grand Rapids, MI: Chosen Books, 1986) page 55-56.

Day 30

1. John Grey, Mars and Venus on a Date (New York, NY: HarperCollins Publishers Inc., 1999) pages 47-48.

Day 31

1. Danny Silk, Keep Your Love On (Redding, CA, Red Arrow Publishing, 2013).
2. Dr. Dan and Linda Wilson, 7 Secrets of a Supernatual Marriage: The Joy of Spirit-Led Intimacy (Racine, WI: Broadstreet Publishing, 2014) pages 2-26.
3. John Eldredge, Brent Curtis, The Sacred Romance, Drawing Closer to the Heart of God (Nashville, TN: Thomas Nelson Publisher, 1997).
4. Jeff Olsen, article in Forbes magazine, 3/17/14.
5. Socrates.

Day 32

1. Waiting Room – Tremelo, Song lyrics by Justin Dillon, Flagship Recordings, 2005.
2. Dr. Norman Vincent Peale, The Power of Positive Thinking (New York, NY, Prentice Hall, Inc. 1952) pages 85-87.

Day 33

1. Climb Every Mountain, song written by Rodgers and Hammerstein, 1958.

Day 34

1. Alison Armstrong, Making Sense of Men (Sherman Oaks, CA, PAX Programs, 2007) page 57-59.

Day 36

1. Ed Silvoso, Transformation (Ventura, CA, Regal Books, 2007) page 247.
2. Mark Twain.

Day 37

1. Charles Capps, God's Creative Power for Finances (England, AR: Capps Publishing, 2004) pages 36-41.

Day 38

1. Beth Moore, So Long Insecurity (Carol Stream, IL: Tyndale House Publishers, Inc., 2010) page 320.

Day 39

1. Man, Word Wealth, New Spirit Filled Life Bible (Nashville, TN, Thomas Nelson Inc., 2002) page 1003.

Day 40

1. Able, Word Wealth, New Spirit Filled Life Bible (Nashville, TN, Thomas Nelson Inc., 2002) page193.
2. Faith When Facing Delays, Kingdom Dynamics, New Spirit Filled Life Bible (Nashville, TN, Thomas Nelson Inc., 2002) page 194.

Testimony from the author

1. Kris Vallotton, http://www.kvministries.com.

END NOTES

12 Days of Christmas

1. Meg Kelsey, Long to Love Blog, December 14, 2011, http://elizabethrobertsonwilliams.com/submitting-to-the-supernatural/
2. Peace, World Wealth, New Spirit Filled Life Bible (Nashville, TN, Thomas Nelson Inc., 2002) page 1218.
3. Kris Vallotton, The Supernatural Ways of Royalty (Shippensburg, PA, Destiny Image, 2006) page 144.
4. Kindness, Word Wealth, New Spirit Filled Life Bible (Nashville, TN, Thomas Nelson Inc., 2002) page 1638.
5. Joy, Word Wealth, New Spirit Filled Life Bible, (Nashville, TN, Thomas Nelson Inc., 2002) page 1228.
6. Patience, Word Wealth, New Spirit Filled Life Bible, (Nashville, TN, Thomas Nelson Inc., 2002) page 1736.
7. Goodness, Word Wealth, New Spirit Filled Life Bible, (Nashville, TN, Thomas Nelson Inc., 2002) page 1573.
8. Faithful, Word Wealth, New Spirit Filled Life Bible, (Nashville, TN, Thomas Nelson Inc., 2002) page 836.
9. Gentleness, Word Wealth, New Spirit Filled Life Bible, (Nashville, TN, Thomas Nelson Inc., 2002) page 1706.
10. Prosper, Word Wealth, New Spirit Filled Life Bible, (Nashville, TN, Thomas Nelson Inc., 2002) page 856.
11. Ed Silvoso, Women: God's Secret Weapon (Bloomington, MN: Chosen Books, 2001) page 113.
12. Sound Mind, Word Wealth, New Spirit Filled Life Bible (Nashville, TN, Thomas Nelson Inc., 2002) page 1711.
13. Fear, Word Wealth, New Spirit Filled Life Bible (Nashville, TN, Thomas Nelson Inc., 2002) page 884.

Appendix A

Appendix B

1. The Right Reverend and Right Honorable Dr. Richard Chartres KCVO, Bishop of London, www.westminster-abbey.org/worship/sermons/2011/april/address-given-at-the-marriage-of-hrh-prince-william-of-wales-with-miss-catherine-middleton.

Appendix C

1. Prayer Ministers: Cutting Yourself Free from Unholy Unions, From the Summer 1997 issue of *The Healing Line Newsletter* (out of print).

www.ingramcontent.com/pod-product-compliance
Lightning Source LLC
Chambersburg PA
CBHW071612080526
44588CB00010B/1107